MORE
HIDDEN
GARDENS

MORE
HIDDEN
GARDENS

Foreword by Chris Beardshaw

Penny David

Photographs by Rowan Isaac

CASSELL
ILLUSTRATED

For John and Sue
and their Hidden Garden

First published in Great Britain in 2004 by Cassell Illustrated,
a division of Octopus Publishing Group Limited
2-4 Heron Quays, London E14 4JP

By arrangement with the BBC
The BBC logo is a registered trademark of the British Broadcasting Corporation
and is used under licence.

BBC logo © BBC 1996
Hidden Gardens © BBC 2002, 2004
Copyright © 2004 Octopus Publishing Group Limited

Text © Penny David 2004
Photographs © Rowan Isaac 2004 apart from those
specified in the picture credits on page 175

A CIP catalogue record for this book is available from the British Library.

1 2 3 4 5 6 7 8 9 10

ISBN 1 84403 215 9

Editorial & design:
Pippa Rubinstein & Judith Robertson,
R & R Publishing
Jacket design: Jo Knowles
Additional picture research: Robin Douglas-Withers & Lisa Thiel
Indexer: Kathie Gill

Printed in Italy

Contents

Hidden in a tangle of highways and high-tech business parks lies an oasis of the natural world, a green garden space whispering with eight centuries of history. Skeletons showing signs of bone disease prompt a quest to re-create the medieval Physic Garden and discover the herbs that might have helped them.

Unseen in the lee of the M5 motorway lies one of Capability Brown's earliest ground breaking landscapes, now being restored in a sweepingly ambitious scheme. There are hundreds of plant bills in the archives: will they dispel for ever the cliché that Brown's designs were flowerless?

A fold in the landscape conceals this curious set of formal gardens, laid out some distance from the owner's house. They are right on the edge of the town but hardly known. As restoration and replanting get them back in shape, what might they reveal about the wealthy Quaker who created them?

Foreword

Throughout history gardeners have been creating gardens that by definition have reflected the needs, whims, and attitudes of the society to which they belong. The gardens referred to in this text and the associated television series span over half a millennium of arguably the most exciting and defining period of gardening and horticulture in Britain. They candidly portray the aims and ambitions of their creators and when viewed individually they provide a remarkable source of stimulation and delight for all the senses, no matter what your gardening persuasion.

However, viewed collectively, they create a perfect encyclopaedia on the art of creating gardens. This holistic approach allows us not only to map the changing face of the art, but also provides an extraordinary source of education and inspiration to modern gardeners. After all, these are the works of some of the most refined, talented and dedicated minds of their day and consequently, despite their historic nature, there are lessons hard learnt by their originators that are just as relevant today.

Most striking is that these diverse gardens are united by one desire — that of creating a garden or landscape that, in the eyes of the creator, represents paradise. Since three and a half thousand years BC, human beings have been using simple walls and fences to create sheltered enclosures in which they could find relief from the stresses of the harsh outside world. The spaces allowed them to modify and adapt their environment for their own pleasure and enjoyment and the art of gardening was born. Over the centuries the nature of the enclosure and the scale and sophistication of the contents may have radically altered, but every gardener, past and present, strives to create their own little piece of Eden. That is after all what 'garden' means.

Chris Beardshaw
December 2003

NORTON PRIORY
A Suitable Case for Physick

'Get me to the priory!' The written instructions are clear: head for Runcorn East and look for the brown signs, for you inevitably come on wheels. Should you forget this and try to follow the road maps – without a competent navigator by your side – you may get driven to distraction. By the time you find the priory you may well need some calming, soothing treatment, some sanctuary.

Norton Priory Museum and Gardens is an oasis after the traffic and the business park where techno-chic buildings with glassy blank expressions sit on smooth lawns amid smug shrubs. The operatives (can you call them gardeners?) who maintain these trim exterior décors might be shocked by the contrasting atmosphere in the wooded priory gardens nearby. Norton Priory gardens are a bosky oasis, a place of deep green shades, where shrubs and trees seem to grow as they please, leaves and petals fall, nature seems to reign.

The brown 'Norton Priory' highway signs are an indication that this garden is not exactly undiscovered. It's much visited and famous locally (Chester, Liverpool and Manchester, all only half-an-hour away, amount to a substantial catchment area). What brings Chris Beardshaw and his *Hidden Gardens* television team to this spot is the potential for an important 'restoration' project. There are eight-and-a-half centuries of garden history to sift through here.

Much has already happened during the last two or three decades. The bones of a medieval priory have been exhumed from beneath many layers of rubble and thicket. Georgian and Victorian garden features have been exposed and repaired – summerhouses, water features, a rockery, an ice house. Ornamental woodland has been reclaimed from rampant rhododendrons and revitalized with new tree and shrub plantings. Today's star attraction is the eighteenth-century walled kitchen garden, which received a major facelift in the 1980s: more a transformation than a renovation.

Now, however, a decision has been made to install an entirely new garden. The idea is to create a garden that would not have been out of place in the days of the medieval priory, the best part of a thousand

An Outline of the Plot

The land of Norton Priory nowadays looks in plan something like an elongated hourglass or egg-timer. Its slim waist is cinched to a hand's span across a busy dual carriageway – the Daresbury Expressway – sunk in a deep cutting below mean ground level. The two unequal halves of the 38-acre (15.4ha) site are linked by a slender bridge over the roadway.

This fragment is all that is left of a once vast estate, but today it possesses wealth of a different kind. Its influence, paradoxically, reaches perhaps greater numbers of people now than at any time, even more than in its medieval prime.

The *raison d'être* of all this lies just to the south of the hourglass waist. Norton Priory (later elevated to Abbey) was built here in 1134 by the Augustinian order and grew in riches and influence for four centuries. After the Dissolution of the Monasteries in 1536, a Tudor house was built on the site and in the mid 1700s it was replaced by a villa in classical mode. By the early twentieth century, as encroaching industrialization blighted the surroundings, the now old-fashioned house was abandoned and the site all but forgotten.

Reawakening came in the 1960s and 1970s. Enlightened officialdom – the Runcorn Development Corporation – decided to create a centre of archaeological and historic interest for the New Town of Runcorn in an area designated as the town park. Archaeologists began excavating the foundations of the priory in 1971, revealing a complex architectural history, while historians complemented their discoveries with documentary research. The priory site opened to the public in 1975, and the Museum building was opened seven years later. Run by the Norton Priory Trust, it has become an award-winning institution. The sheer number and quality of the artefacts found here has gained high marks in scholarly circles. The excellence of the amenities and facilities – and the high standard of interpretation – earns the warm approval of the vast number of visitors.

'Woman Planting'
by Christine Kowal Post.

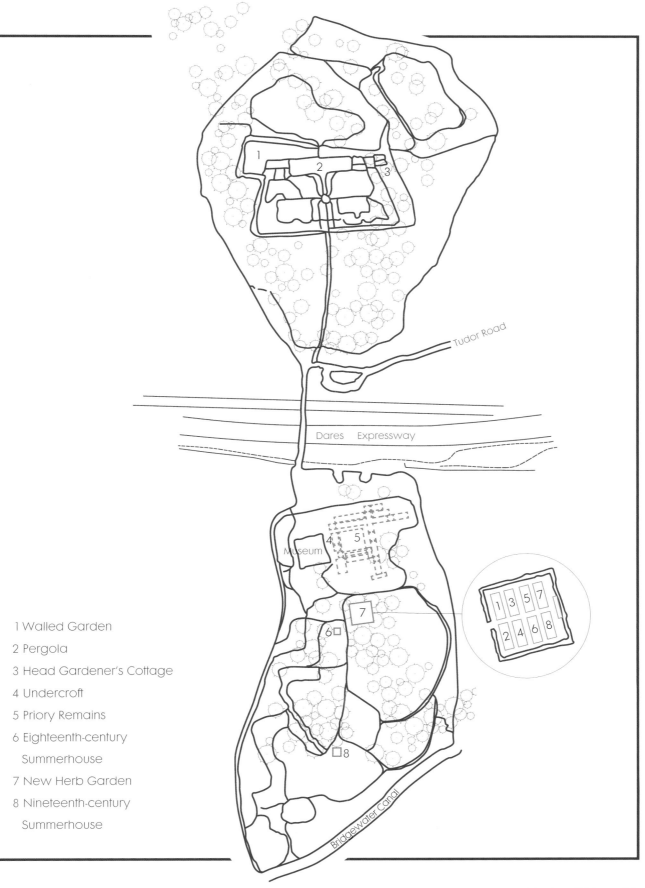

1 Walled Garden

2 Pergola

3 Head Gardener's Cottage

4 Undercroft

5 Priory Remains

6 Eighteenth-century
  Summerhouse

7 New Herb Garden

8 Nineteenth-century
  Summerhouse

Tudor Road

Dares Expressway

Museum

Bridgewater Canal

years ago. A key is the priory's traditional role in caring for the sick. A medieval physic garden seems entirely fitting, but how will they set about it, since no plans exist?

It is worth listening, too, to the language people use to describe the business of bringing the past back to life. It is not just what you do but the way you talk about it. Reconstruction, restoration and re-creation are three approaches that one expert has distinguished for reviving historic gardens. Which one will apply here?

A Sense of the Past

Interpreting a site like Norton Priory is a challenge. The museum must provide a positive 'visitor experience', but must also explain the layered past. The Georgian house that stood here almost within living memory was a 'recent' item, surplus to requirements in the twentieth century, and replaced an unfashionable older Tudor building. Both, however, were built on the site of the Augustinian priory, and both incorporated fragments of the older buildings. Working backwards from today, all that the three earlier stages of Norton Priory have in common is the undercroft, later used as an entrance hall. Those of us who studied history at school know at least that the Middle Ages come before the Tudors and Stuarts, and that then there's a neatly numbered series of Georges for a century or so. (It helps to picture people dressed like Shakespeare walking about in the Tudor house, or Jane Austen characters in the later one.) But in spite of this useful timeline it's hard to think spatially and to imagine in three dimensions how lost buildings filled a space. And when such vast and long-lived buildings have evaporated into thin air, how much harder is it to envisage the succession of ephemeral gardens that enhanced them?

Peel back the layers. 'Start with what you know,' is the advice of Lynn Smith, Senior Keeper at Norton. One living link is with the Brooke family, who bought the estate after the Dissolution and who continue to be involved with the priory in its contemporary role. Local people have personal or family reminiscences or associations with the site. Strangers to the site – visitors – need to be offered some grasp of the historical record. But it is the medieval origins of the priory that are principally evoked in the museum area.

Both scholars and schoolchildren ask 'How long did the Middle Ages last?' and 'How dark were the Dark Ages?' These are valid questions. It is worth reminding ourselves that the subject of medieval religious houses, too, is diverse and complex. Although there were some patterns, there were many different rules, which developed over time, and surviving evidence is sometimes patchy. We do, however, know a fair bit about Norton Priory.

Lynn Smith points out some of the highlights of Norton's artistic heritage. There is the oversized statue of St Christopher, a first-class piece of sculpture and a unique survival. A modern stained-glass window recaptures its brilliant medieval appearance, when it would have been painted with bright and costly pigments. On a smaller scale entirely are some of the decorations on glazed terracotta tiles. The vine motif has been adopted as the logo of the Norton Priory Trust. It is a reminder of the warmer climate during the period, broadly from 1150 to 1300, when substantial amounts of wine were made in England and dessert grapes were grown. Subtler still are the carvings on some of the stone coffin lids displayed in the museum. One has the spreading leaves and stems of a vine, bursting with energy. Another represents a tree-of-life motif. Like the tiles, these have the vigour of direct observation, as in the rare early herbals where an artist has drawn from nature rather than merely copying.

One way to 'get in touch' with our medieval forebears is through plants – by means of herbs and the senses they evoke. When we squeeze a filament-leaf of fennel between our fingers we release the same aniseed aroma that must have tickled the nostrils of the Norton canons. When we hear the buzz of bees as they assault the nectar-rich flowers of hyssop on a sunny day, we're hearing a sound that would have pleased them too, with its promise of stores of honey for sweet-ness and beeswax for light. They would not have understood the process of pollination, but might have admired the industry of the bee as it reflected the wonders of God's creation.

In the abbey's heyday the statue was painted in expensive pigments – the colour of its red robes derived from mercury and its green trousers from crushed bronze verdigris. A modern stained-glass window recalls this lost glory. St Christopher, patron saint of travellers, was significant for visitors to Norton Abbey who would wish for a safe crossing of the Mersey 3 miles (5km) away.

Norton Priory was an Augustinian foundation. Our homework tells us that of the two possible Saints Augustine, Norton's is St Augustine of Hippo – who wrote the *Confessions* – not the Saint Augustine of Canterbury. He was born in 354 in what is now Tunisia. His father was a pagan; his mother was a Christian (later sanctified as St Monica). At Carthage, where he went to study, he encountered new intellectual climates and temptations of the flesh, and he fathered a son, Adeonatus.

He taught in Rome and Milan, was baptized as a Christian, and returned to North Africa. He was made Bishop of Hippo in 396 and died in 430 as the Vandals were besieging the gates of the city.

'Give me chastity and continency, but not yet.'

St Augustine

When his sister entered a religious community, Augustine sent her his thoughts on chastity, charity and concord, and the contents of his letter later became the basis of the Rule of St Augustine, developed in Europe in the twelfth century. Augustinian or Austin canons took religious vows like monks, but were less isolated from the outside world. They made clerical and parochial duties their predominant obligation and, like other religious orders, they were a repository of knowledge. Their scribes in the scriptorium would unquestioningly copy the received wisdom contained in ancient texts of scriptures and herbals. Healing and nursing the sick would form an important element of the work of the community. Hospitality in the modern sense would be offered, and prayers, and Norton must have represented a special staging post for travellers taking the ferry across the river Mersey 3 miles (5km) away. The priory, incidentally, received a tithe of the profits from the ferry crossing, so had a special interest in passengers' wellbeing. The statue of St Christopher symbolizes this aspect of Norton Priory.

At the heart of the museum at Norton Priory are the bones of a monastic building and the skeleton of one of its inmates in his stone coffin. Stripped bare, their stark shapes seem to represent how little we know of their lives. But both have extraordinary stories to tell. Let's start with the stones, the building itself. (Skeletons will speak later.)

The footings of the priory walls run this way and that, delineating rectangles through panels of mown grass in the manner of hundreds

Norton's graves were made for prestigious lay people as well as the canons themselves. Only the wealthiest benefactors of Norton Priory (or Abbey) would have been in a position to commission chiselled stone coffins to contain the mortal remains of their loved ones, or to dictate where in the ecclesiastical layout they might be buried. This grouping is of a man and three children.

Ever since Sir Richard Brooke purchased the abbey estates in 1545, the Brooke family has been closely connected with Norton. Although they moved to Worcestershire in the 1920s, members of the family continue to give active support to Norton Priory and its concerns in its new incarnation.

of heritage sites commemorating lost medieval buildings all over Britain. By reading the shapes – and because such religious foundations usually conformed to a pattern – experts have been able to identify areas such as the cloister garden and its surrounding walk, the church, chapter house, refectory range and so on. It is a challenge as you walk between the stony outlines in the open air to conjure the lofty spaces that were once enclosed by these invisible walls.

It is harder still to envisage the lives of the men who created this place, lived here, and became some of the skeletons. The core inhabitants were the prior or abbot, perhaps twenty-four 'Black Canons' (so called for the colour of their habits) and their servants. If you carry in your head the Gregorian chant playing faintly in the museum display area, you may gain some hint at a definition of the church with its atmosphere of echoing song. Inside the museum substantial scale models show the priory buildings as they were – at least, at key stages in their chequered evolution. We should recall that Norton Priory stood on this spot for almost exactly four centuries. The original house was founded at Runcorn in 1115, but the prior and canons moved to Norton in 1134. Their successors were moved out in 1536. A great deal happens in four hundred years: after all, that's the period that has elapsed between the death of Elizabeth I and our own time. After one hundred years the church and cloister burned down and were rebuilt. In the 1390s the priory was given the rare distinction – rare for an Augustinian house in England – of being raised to abbey status. Depredations by natural disasters like fire and flood were offset by the gifts that flowed in from wealthy patrons and landowners. In its heyday Norton owned estates and property in many Midlands counties, and no doubt the fabric of the priory reflected some of this wealth. Augustinians led a life that was not too austere. It seems they ate well, and the interior of their church was colourful and bejewelled. Perhaps the abbot's tower looked down on to well-stocked scent-filled gardens.

This life all came to a sudden end with Henry VIII's Dissolution of the Monasteries.

The House After Henry

When Henry VIII dissolved the monasteries in 1536, Norton Abbey was one of the first to go. Its plate and other valuables were confiscated and the canons dispersed. In 1545 Sir Richard Brooke, a prominent local landowner from Leighton, near Crewe, bought the abbey and its estates for £1512 1s 9d. He converted the west range or outer courtyard buildings and the abbot's tower into a house, demolishing the church and the other buildings surrounding the cloister, but retaining the gatehouse. The offices such as brewhouse, bakehouse, dairy, slaughterhouse, barn and stables that had served the canons continued their original functions in this new secular age. The Buck brothers' engraving of 1727 shows a sprawling half-timbered house extending from the abbey's remains, a natural, organic growth. We can picture its interior with the dark oak of the panelling, the generous staircase with newel posts polished by generations of hands, the wide floorboards, and the strapwork plaster ceilings, and some of us would give our eyeteeth to see it again: all too few houses remain from this age. Outside, gardens of similarly fine quality followed the rectilinear pattern of earlier enclosures, moats and millponds. Gradually they would be decorated and coloured with new introductions: nasturtiums from the New World, tulips from Turkey, pelargoniums from the Cape.

Two centuries later the rambling Tudor house had in turn disappeared. Fashion in the mid eighteenth century dictated the building

The brothers Samuel and Nathaniel Buck toured England and Wales depicting historic buildings with an almost photographic accuracy that has provided historians with an invaluable resource ever since. Their engraving of Norton in 1727 shows a sprawling half-timbered house extending from the abbey remains. Just distinguishable in the second archway to the right of the stairway is the statue of St Christopher.

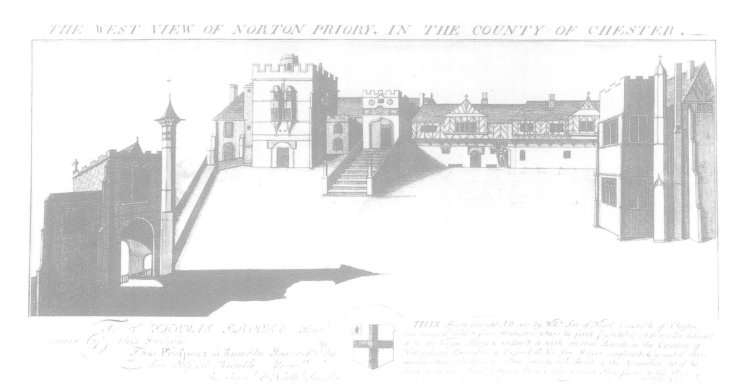

THE WEST VIEW OF NORTON PRIORY, IN THE COUNTY OF CHESTER.

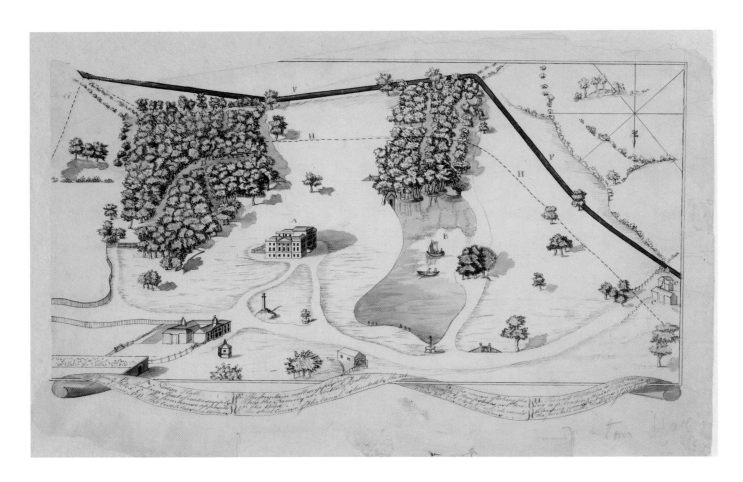

This bird's-eye view of the 'new' Georgian house taken in the 1770s (with north towards the bottom of the view) shows the millpond transformed into a boating lake. A temple, boathouse and Chinese bridge are half hidden in the wood. A corner of the existing kitchen garden is visible in the foreground, but the stables and dovecote seen have since disappeared. The Brooke family had this perspective drawn to contest the Duke of Bridgewater's plans to cut a canal through their pleasure grounds.

of a new dwelling in classical style. The medieval undercroft was incorporated into the new house and used for storage. Later in the century the architect James Wyatt is reputed to have made some alterations to the house, and he may have designed the small classical summerhouse that still stands in the grounds.

By about 1770 the gardens and moats that still existed in 1757 had been swept away and 'Norton Hall' sat resplendent amid landscaped pleasure grounds, with lawns to the doorstep, the millpond converted to a boating lake and the introduction of eyecatchers including dovecote, temple and chinoiserie bridge. The Georgian house looks neat enough in prints of the time but is one of a type, lacking the vigour and individuality of its Tudor predecessor. In the grounds the streams first made waterfalls and a small lake, and then formed two stream glades that still exist. The present path system had been established by the early nineteenth century. Further changes were made to the house in the 1860s, when part of the undercroft was turned into an entrance hall. These alterations made use of a romanesque doorway dating from about 1180–1200 that had probably formed the entrance to the nave of the church from the west cloister walk. The doorway was, however, rather small for the purpose. With perfect Victorian aplomb, a replica of the original was commissioned and made, and the two archways still stand side by side, inviting the visitor to guess 'which is which'.

Not everything was rosy. The outside world had a way of impinging on private estates. The Brookes were unhappy in the 1770s when the Duke of Bridgewater planned to cut a canal through their pleasure grounds. In spite of their reasoned remonstrations, the canal went ahead and was completed in 1776. The canal altered the water balance of the area, although Brooke took his streams by culvert under the canal. Later, in the early nineteenth century, the family was more successful in having the Halton–Warrington road diverted to the north to avoid the inconvenience of traffic passing close to the house.

Outdoors, early photographs show a return to Victorian formality in the gardens near the house. The surrounding estate was described

Overlooking the new herb garden is a neat classical building that dates from the late eighteenth century. The small summerhouse may have been built by the architect James Wyatt, who is supposed to have been making some alterations to the Georgian house at the time.

as one of the finest in Cheshire: 'The magnificence of its oaks was notorious, all the trees, shrubs, hedges, etc were healthy and sound and the soil being good the land produced satisfactory and profitable crops.' By the 1920s the Victorianized Georgian house had in turn become outmoded. More seriously, advancing industry had marred its rural setting. Complaints began as early as 1870:

> When the wind is in the northwest… the windows of the mansion cannot be opened… because of the smell that immediately fills the house and people walking in the park, even those who have grown accustomed to the sickening smell, suffer from a smarting or pricking sensation in the eyes. The greenhouse and hothouse doors cannot be opened with impunity…much damage might be done in a short time.

It all became too much. The Brooke family moved to Abberley, near Worcester, in 1921. The house was later demolished in 1928.

Palimpsest and Pastiche

Restoration people sometimes describe historic gardens as a palimpsest. A palimpsest is literally a writing surface or a parchment, flayed from the skin of a lamb, calf or kid, which has been scraped clean so that the material can be reused. The original writing was not

This photograph of the modified Georgian house in around 1900 shows a return to Victorian formality in the gardens near the house. The venerable statue of St Christopher can be seen making a garden focal point at far right.

always perfectly effaced, so it has sometimes been possible to recover works that were otherwise lost.

At Norton successive secular houses in all their material splendour have risen and gone, leaving the footings of the original religious buildings visible on the ground. Norton is a figurative palimpsest, a surface once again laid bare, where we can trace a message that was almost lost. The spirit of St Augustine comes to mind, with its spiritual questioning and humanity – a fitting parallel. Augustine read Cicero and Plato in his quest for truth. On an actual palimpsest – a recycled parchment of Cicero's *De Republica* – he wrote a commentary on the psalms. But the words of the Roman statesman were not entirely erased, and it has been possible to recover and study them from beneath Augustine's script. What has become hidden may yet be revealed.

The palimpsest provides a useful metaphor for historians, but in reality a garden often leaves no trace that it ever existed. In her book *The Medieval Garden* Sylvia Landsberg distinguishes three approaches to historical garden design: *reconstruction*, where sufficient evidence exists about a past garden to enable an identical layout to be brought to life; *restoration*, where sufficient remains have survived to enable the garden to be returned to its former glory; and *re-creation*, sometimes known as pastiche.

The large summerhouse among the trees not far from the canal was built in 1829. In contrast to the classical summerhouse on page 21, it was built in rustic style with rough stone walls and leaded windows. Both, however, serve as touchstones that allow visitors to appreciate an important period in Norton's past of which most tangible evidence has simply disappeared.

The last, she maintains, is the only option for medieval gardens, where no garden is known to have existed on the site but 'enough is known about other gardens of the time to assemble a jigsaw of the most common features'. This has to be the case at Norton Priory, where they must have had gardens but nothing remains of them. It is a pity the word 'pastiche' has such pejorative overtones, but there are contexts where a pastiche may be worthwhile.

Here's One We Restored Earlier

The 2.4 acre (0.97ha) Georgian walled garden is the jewel in Norton's garden crown, a byword for one option in garden restoration. Or, as Sylvia Landsberg might say, pastiche?

They built the walled garden around 1770. For 150 years it fulfilled its role of feeding the Brooke family and their household, but with the twentieth century came redundancy, a likely fate even if the house had not been abandoned. By the time a rescue bid was launched in the 1980s the walls were hidden in vegetation and the head gardener's cottage was tumbling down. The local authority provided funds. The hard structures were rebuilt. A decision was taken not to restore the range of glasshouses on the sunny side of the north wall, but instead to replace them with a creative alternative, a modern solution. A vast ornamental pergola built in brick runs along the north wall, providing a sense of containment that echoes the lost glasshouse enclosures but serves a different purpose. Swathed in climbing plants, it provides people with shade rather than plants with protection.

The design of the open ground respects the original plan of dividing the garden into four quarters, but the subdivisions are put to different and non-historical uses. There are vegetable plots, a herb garden, an orchard, an apple tunnel and the National Collection of quince trees, *Cydonia oblonga* – the original marmalade fruit. But many of the areas are designed as small, separate enclosures to give visitors inspiration for their own domestic gardens. The planting is gorgeous and the herbaceous borders in summer are breathtaking.

The refurbishment included commissioning a new wrought-iron gate for the south wall, the grand entrance for people of the past who approached from the Hall. Actually, human visitors don't use the iron gate: we enter through the rebuilt head gardener's house, which has displays telling the story of the garden's rescue, and bundles of rhubarb (or whatever is in season) for sale. The garden is not geared to full-scale crop production, but these tokens are an important part of the mission to keep the past alive.

The inspiration for the new south gate was the tree of life. The idea echoes the tree carved in stone on one of Norton's coffin lids, and marks Norton's theme of 'recycling' inspiration. The artist placed little wrought-iron rabbits in the foreground of the gate. Real little furry rabbits squeezed through the gaps, so wire mesh had to be attached. Today's garden staff watch in dismay as a race of super-rabbits learns to vault through gaps above the mesh. The sights and smells within the garden are enough to entice anyone in.

Perhaps these are the descendants of the rabbits who made an earlier comeback in Norman times, around the period when Norton Priory was in the building. They had originally been brought to Britain by the Romans but succumbed to hungry dark-age predators. Now warrens – or coneygarths – were established by lords of the manor (and heads of religious houses) to provide meat. An adult rabbit was known as a coney; the name 'rabbit' was used only for animals less than a year old. We should issue a warning here for readers of a delicate disposition who find Mr MacGregor upsetting. Most prized by the medieval epicure were 'rabbit suckers' or *laurices*, suckling (or even

The wrought-iron gate for the main entrance in the south wall was designed by Dianne Gorvin. It provides an inviting glimpse into the garden, but today's visitors must continue around the perimeter and enter through the head gardener's cottage.

unborn) baby rabbits. The flesh of suckling rabbits was 'singularly praised in physic; for all things the which doth suck is nutritive'. For monks they had a special appeal: they were deemed 'not meat' and could be eaten on fast days (just as beavers, as water-dwellers, were regarded as fish by Catholic colonists of North America).

Inevitably there were escapees, and since more land was in cultivation there were fewer predators. They bred, as we know, like rabbits. And they still do, although very few of them are known to improve the diet of the humans who frequent Norton Priory nowadays.

Dead Men's Bones

It's not all glamour, being a television presenter. Like gardening itself it takes hard work, a gritty, down-to-earth attitude, good all-round knowledge and a degree of versatility. Disciplines that don't usually feature on the gardener's CV are dentistry and paleopathology.

Bones have various uses in horticultural contexts in the guise of bonemeal, or blood, fish and bone. Old gardeners used knobbly animal bones to edge their beds and make decorative floors for garden huts. You sometimes buried a whole domestic or farm animal in the spot where you were going to plant a vine – providing slow-release fertilizer of the most basic kind. But studying human skeletons is not usually on the gardener's agenda. The Norton Priory project takes Chris Beardshaw to Bradford University to meet paleopathologist Anthea Boylston and dentist Alan Ogden who have studied the skeletal remains exhumed during the priory excavations. What do the bones tell them?

Typical of a monastic site is the large proportion of elderly males. It was not unusual to reach a ripe old age if you managed to survive the rigours of childhood. The state of many of the skeletons indicates a healthy and comfortable lifestyle. Anthea Boylston notes that there are comparatively few fractures. Active individuals, like soldiers, often had broken bones in leg or foot because they were constantly travelling over rough ground; old or infirm people who fell often had broken ribs. Most Norton skeletons also had surprisingly good teeth: 'A lifetime of

The rebuilt head gardener's cottage contains offices and a display showing the history of the walled garden and the story of its rescue. The nearby planting inside the garden is informal and cottagy in style.

chewing with great gusto,' is Alan Ogden's comment. Worn down, yes, by the grit incorporated when grain was milled for flour; but showing none of the destruction of enamel caused by acid/plaque interaction: little refined carbohydrate in the diet, and cane sugar in only the tiniest amounts, for the very top echelon.

Not all the Norton skeletons were canons. Some belong to the wealthy families – the barons of Halton and the Duttons – who were patrons and benefactors of the priory, which accounts for the quota of women and children found in certain areas. Wills made by members of the Dutton family requested burial under the lady chapel, and in return masses would be said for their souls in perpetuity. The location of the skeletons corroborates this documentary evidence: most of the elderly males – the canons – were found buried under the nave or the cloister walk. The gradation of privilege you find in the burials reflects that of society. The nearer you were to the heart of the church, the healthier and better fed the people must have been. The further away, the more likely you were to have had a poorer diet, the more diseases you might have had, the lower your social status, the harder your life.

Anthea Boylston points out other skeletons showing signs of disease that suggest that the priory was providing some kind of hospital service to the community. One individual has deformations of the collar bone and ribs – and of a finger – that suggest he died of tuberculosis; his skull and his teeth confirm he was a young adult, in his twenties or thirties. Dentist Alan Ogden steps in with the tale of the teeth. Grooving in the front teeth – uneven growth when the enamel was forming in childhood – indicates that this young man had four severe bouts of childhood illness. This must have reduced his immune system and made him more susceptible to a disease that has been endemic in Britain since Roman times. 'It's educated guesswork, using the clues you can find to build up a consistent picture.'

Many of the plants we grow as ornamentals were once used for medicinal or other purposes. In today's more cautious climate plant labels and seed packets often carry health warnings, and the public is warned not to experiment even with apparently harmless herbs.

All-heal.
Boneset. Bruisewort.
Coughwort. Cure-all.
Feverfew. Goutweed.
Knitbone.
Live-for-ever.
Lousewort. Lungwort.
Piss-a-bed. Scabwort.
Woundwort.

Old common names for herbs

What treatment might the canons have offered? Drinking an infusion of goosegrass or cleavers ('which are recognized by their round seed which adhere to the clothes when ripe') was one medieval remedy. Other recommended medicinal herbs were agrimony, betony, centaury, comfrey, elecampane, horehound, hyssop, pennyroyal, plantain, rue and sage, but how they were to be taken is not specified.

One of the inmates of the infirmary died of leprosy: the collapse of the bone structure of the face is the clue. The bacillus likes cold parts of the body, we learn, hence its concentration on the extremities, and the air-cooled nose and mouth area. How might the canons have treated this character? The disease would have looked to them like a skin complaint, so they might have applied poultices. This would have had no effect on the condition as a whole, but could have eased the problems of secondary wounds and infections afflicting areas where the sufferer had lost the sense of feeling. More important, perhaps, would have been the therapeutic, palliative aspect of the treatment, since leprosy bore a social stigma. Anise, marsh mallow, melissa, mint,

Coffins carved in stone attest to the wealth and rank of the people buried at Norton. Bones, now preserved elsewhere, can reveal information about their general health and their diseases. The rest, such as how their ailments were treated, must be conjecture. Many medieval treatments consisted of faith and fancy in equal measures.

wallflower and woodsage appear on some lists. Their contemporaries in Wales, the lay Physicians of Myddfai, recommended a decoction of burdock, taken internally and applied externally. Alternatively:

> Get the roots of the red dock, the roots of the elecampane, honeysuckle leaves, wild hyacinth, broom sprigs, bugle, violet, heath shieldfern, and avens; pound them well together in a mortar with unsalted butter, boiling them well, removing from the fire and straining through new linen; add thereto a portion of flour of brimstone and verdigris…

Most of these ingredients would grow as wild plants rather than garden crops (wild hyacinth is bluebell), which is all fascinating but of little help with suggestions for the planting of Norton Priory's projected new physic garden.

A surprise discovery is that no fewer than six of the Norton Priory skeletons display signs of Paget's disease, *Osteitis deformans*, in which parts of the bones become overcalcified and dense, while other parts become demineralized (and 'look like cottonwool' on X-ray). Paget's is a metabolic disease, possibly with a genetic pattern, described in Victoria's reign by Sir James Paget. This early cluster of cases should be interesting for epidemiologists. You find sporadic cases in other cemeteries, but Anthea Boylston has never seen this number in one site. Neighbouring Lancashire is already recognized as a kind of hotspot for the disease.

'Anoint the diseased part with this ointment and by God's help it will cure it.'

Physicians of Myddfai

As with the leprosy, the canons' principal treatment would have been palliative. 'I think the picture you get is that their medicaments may not have done much about the root cause of the condition, but they may have been effective at reducing inflammation and soothing the wounds,' says Alan Ogden. 'And there's always the element that people automatically feel better if something is being done, if they are being cared for.' Pressed by Chris Beardshaw for herbs that might have been used, one suggestion is garlic, with its antibiotic effects. Lichen and toadstools are too unspecific. Then Alan recalls reading recently about a soothing lotion made from marigold heads.

So at last we have two potential items for the planting list: garlic and marigold. That's pot marigold, *Calendula officinalis*, reintroduced in the early Middle Ages (and featured in homeopathic treatment today), not the parvenu *Tagetes* species that came from the New World only after Columbus, somehow accruing the adjective French or African on the way. At least marigold is garden-worthy: it is pretty, and long-flowering and so named because, according to some, it bloomed on the calends (the first day) of every month.

Obviously the bones cannot give us the complete picture. There were many other ailments that don't manifest themselves in the skeletons. But the skeletons have survived, and they provide that vital starting point.

A Note on the Practice

The monastic tradition of healing evolved. The zealous Pope Innocent III (pope between 1198 and 1216) ruled that no ecclesiastic should practise medicine for private gain or shed blood in any way. As a result

Norton's Walled Garden contains a wide range of 'sub-gardens' including an orchard and demonstration plots given a range of different treatments. This is the herb garden, a decorative layout containing beds of herbs for culinary, medicinal and household use.

some of the monks who worked in physic gardens renounced their vows and continued to practise as laymen. They became apothecaries. They might work as what were later known as itinerant 'quacksalvers' or quacks, gathering simples (medicinal herbs) and selling their own compounds, or might settle down in one place, perhaps growing their own herbs, and set up shop. (The epithet *officinalis* or *officinale* that we find so often in the botanical names of herbs means precisely 'of the shop' – they were available in apothecaries' shops.) Since monks were no longer able to treat or operate on patients, their surgical role too was passed to laymen – often barbers. A deep and long-lasting split began to form between the different aspects of medicine. The physicians became increasingly preoccupied with theory, effecting a diagnosis by studying specimens and casting horoscopes and then directing the patient to the surgeon or the apothecary for the appropriate practical treatment.

Norton's New Herb Garden

Visitors familiar with the pretty gardens illuminated in medieval manuscripts and books of hours may find the severity of an authentic design something of a shock, although in time the maturing herbs will soften the stark plan. The layout of the new herb garden is based on a manuscript plan found in the library at the monastery of St Gall in Switzerland and dating from about AD 820, which included a vegetable garden, a cemetery cum orchard, and a small medicinal garden near the physician's house. It is functional in the extreme. Eight rectangular beds surrounded by an enclosure of willow hurdles

Tom Dagnall's figure 'The Kneeling Monk' (1987) presides over the creation of the new herb garden.

Medieval Times Tables for Medicinal Fluid Measures

4 podfuls = 1 spoonful.

4 spoonfuls = 1 eggshellful.

4 eggshellfuls = 1 cupful.

4 cupfuls = 1 quart.

4 quarts = 1 gallon.

4 grains of wheat = 1 pea.

4 peas = 1 acorn.

4 acorns = 1 pigeon's egg.

4 pigeon's eggs = 1 hen's egg.

4 hen's eggs = 1 goose's egg.

4 goose's eggs = 1 swan's egg.

have been planted with herbs that the priory canons would have known. Each of the beds has a separate theme: culinary herbs, dye plants and strewing herbs are self-explanatory. One bed illustrates the Doctrine of Signatures, the idea that 'like cured like' and contains herbs like lungwort, thought to benefit the lungs, and mandrake with its anthropomorphic root. Four of the beds are specially themed to suit Norton's role as a medieval hospital or hospice. They are thought-provokingly planted with some of the herbs that were used to treat particular maladies: leprosy, Paget's disease, rickets and tuberculosis.

In the end Norton's new herb garden must be described as pastiche. Some herbs transcend categorization. Sage, for instance, is culinary, medicinal and has household virtues. Herbs used as dyestuffs are an additional category in the garden, and the separate beds planted with herbs to treat specific diseases are not particularly authentic.

What the scheme does succeed in doing is putting across to visitors the message of how dependent medieval people were on a fairly limited

Above Ranger Paul Quigley wheels another barrowload of new herb plants past the eighteenth-century classical summerhouse.

Left Gardener John Budworth holds a fencing post while Ranger Sarah Barwick wields the sledge hammer.

Norton's New Medieval Herb Garden

The overall design of the new herb garden is derived from the historic St Gall plan. However, the medieval herbs planted in each of the eight rectangular beds have been chosen for their special significance to the history of Norton Priory and its wider community.

Bed 1 Culinary herbs

Coriander *Coriandrum sativum*

Fennel *Foeniculum vulgare*

Common mallow *Malva sylvestris*

Parsley *Petroselinum crispum*

Rosemary *Rosmarinus officinalis*

Sage *Salvia officinalis*

Thyme *Thymus vulgaris*

Rosa Mundi *Rosa gallica* 'Versicolor'

Bed 2 Doctrine of Signatures

Figwort (glands) *Scrophularia nodosa*

Greater celandine (liver) *Chelidonium majus*

Herb Robert (head wounds) *Geranium robertianum*

Lesser celandine (piles) *Ranunculus ficaria*

Lungwort (lungs) *Pulmonaria officinalis*

Mandrake (human form) *Mandragora officinarum*

Apothecary's rose *Rosa gallica officinalis*

Bed 3 Paget's disease

Clary sage *Salvia sclarea*

Fennel *Foeniculum vulgare*

Melilot *Melilotus officinalis*

Mint *Mentha spicata*

Pennyroyal *Mentha pulegium*

Mullein *Verbascum thapsus*

Rosa 'Great Maiden's Blush'

Bed 4 Tuberculosis

Coriander *Coriandrum sativum*

Elecampane *Inula helenium*

Figwort *Scrophularia nodosa*

Garlic *Allium sativum*

Horehound *Marrubium vulgare*

Houseleek *Sempervivum tectorum*

Madonna lily *Lilium candidum*

Lovage *Levisticum officinale*

Rose 'Quatre Saisons' *Rosa x damascena semperflorens*

Bed 5 Rickets

Anise *Pimpinella anisum*

Betony *Stachys officinale*

Comfrey *Symphytum officinale*

Rue *Ruta graveolens*

Valerian *Valeriana officinalis*

Vervain *Verbena officinalis*

Rosa x *damascena versicolor*

Bed 6 Leprosy

Hyssop *Hyssopus officinalis*

Juniper *Juniperus communis*

Lemon balm *Melissa officinalis*

Common mallow *Malva sylvestris*

Marshmallow *Althaea officinalis*

Sage *Salvia officinalis*

Thyme *Thymus vulgaris*

Rosa eglanteria

Bed 7 Dye plants

Agrimony *Agrimonia eupatoria*

Betony *Stachys officinalis*

Dyer's bugloss *Alkanna tinctoria*

Madder *Rubia tinctorum*

Pennyroyal *Mentha pulegium*

Weld *Reseda luteola*

Woad *Isatis tinctoria*

Rosa x *alba* 'Alba Semiplena'

Bed 8 Strewing herbs

Lavender *Lavandula angustifolia*

Lemon balm *Melissa officinalis*

Mint *Mentha spicata*

Mugwort *Artemisia vulgaris*

Alecost or Tansy *Tanacetum balsamiia*

Woodruff *Galium odoratum*

Rosa x *alba* 'Alba Semiplena'

range of plant materials from the Old World. If we see it as an aid to communication, a discussion forum, then we are in direct touch with one aspect of our forebears. The Austin canons and their lay helpers would have grown many of their herbs elsewhere in quantity, as crops; but they would also have had their demonstration garden where novices would learn to recognize and name the different herbs, and learn their supposed properties by rote.

One aspect of the museum's interpretation brief will surely be fulfilled. The living herbs will act as a *memento mori*, sending visitors back to the stone coffins around the ruins and into the medieval time capsule inside the museum with new consideration for and curiosity about the people who haunted this spot all those centuries ago.

Above and Below Under the twinkling eyes of the kneeling monk, everyone lends a hand with planting up the herb beds including Brian, Philip, John and Richard of Astmoor Day Services, under the guidance of Neil Warburton.

Right Herb expert Jekka McVicar drove up to Norton Priory to deliver in person some of the more unusual herbs on the planting list – all species known in the Middle Ages. She and Chris Beardshaw discuss some of the confusions over the changing names of herbs.

CROOME PARK
Discovering Concealed Capabilities

 Cue Chris Beardshaw on the skyline recording a piece to camera. 'This must be the most visited garden in the world: every year thirty-six million of us pass right through the very heart of it, but we don't realize it's there,' he says. The camera pans away and shows a less than horticultural setting: a bridge over a motorway. The background white noise of traffic becomes clearer. 'In the 1960s the M5 was driven right through here, slicing in two one of our most important landscapes. This is Croome Park.' Strangers to their surroundings, the unknowing garden visitors are driving along the M5, between junctions 7 and 8, where it joins the M50. The motorway cuts right down through the western edge of the park, usurping its beautiful borrowed landscape of the Malvern Hills on the western horizon.

Apart from the motorway, Croome Park is one of those most English of English landscapes. It is the earliest creation of that eighteenth-century genius Lancelot 'Capability' Brown in a career in that changed the face of much of the country. As your eye caresses its familiar, easy contours, pastoral images escape their chocolate-box clichés and come alive. You might even hear in your mind or from the television the soaring orchestral strings of essentially English music. This is Elgar country. The Severn valley. The heart of England. You could almost say that the heart of England cliché was coined here 250 years ago, when a young jobbing architect created an epitome of the river Severn at the command of an ambitious young landowner. (What mental pictures would Elgar's music evoke without Brown's landscape?)

This is also Beardshaw country. Chris grew up near here, at Pershore, a bike ride away, and the majestic oaks and decaying buildings hidden in this landscape were fun to explore. Here were sown the seeds of a deeper curiosity. That curiosity is blossoming now, and from his knowledge of garden history Chris gives us perspectives on the hidden history of Croome Park.

The task of restoring Croome raises questions of perception: how different is what we now see as a 'Capability' Brown landscape from

An Outline of the Plot

Croome Park is one of the most significant landscapes in England. Its design was commissioned by the sixth Earl of Coventry, who pursued a vast programme of landscape improvement from 1747 until his death in 1809. Lord Coventry employed a great number of distinguished architects and craftsmen at Croome, but it is for the pioneering work by Lancelot 'Capability' Brown (1715–83) that Croome is most renowned. At Croome Brown established the English Landscape Style that was to be admired and copied throughout the western world, and in turn Croome made Brown's reputation.

The combination of beauty and economic efficiency – a vision of ideal nature – that characterized Croome in its heyday has faded with time, and in recent decades modern land management has undone much of the texture and detail of the design.

The Rotunda

The Croome Estate Trust and the Coventry family maintained the estate until 1981. Today Croome Court is now in private ownership. The National Trust bought 670 acres of the designed landscape in 1996. Now, in its most ambitious garden restoration project to date, the Trust is tackling the huge task of returning Croome Park to its former glory – to the way it looked as it matured around 1800. Buildings and statues are being restored. The lake and river are being cleared of choking weeds. Trees and acres of shrubbery are being replanted. Grazing rather than arable farming will re-create the green pasture that links the elements into a whole.

Behind this restoration work lies a wealth of expertise. Together with the wonderful estate records and archives maintained by the Croome Estate Trustees, the project is revealing all sorts of hidden knowledge and adding volumes to our understanding of the making of the eighteenth-century landscape.

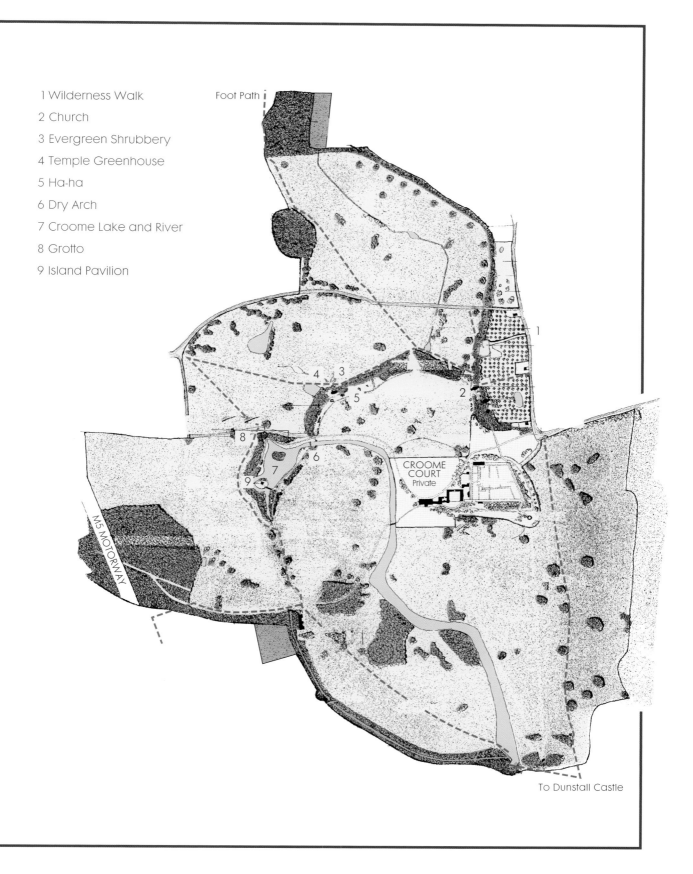

1 Wilderness Walk

2 Church

3 Evergreen Shrubbery

4 Temple Greenhouse

5 Ha-ha

6 Dry Arch

7 Croome Lake and River

8 Grotto

9 Island Pavilion

Foot Path

M5 MOTORWAY

CROOME COURT Private

To Dunstall Castle

the original? Perhaps more than anything, this restoration helps to reveal a huge hidden world, the labour and the loss that went into the making of these apparently glorious landscapes of the eighteenth century. Our chapter follows two 'hidden' themes: what lies beneath the surface, and the plantings that have disappeared but characterized the authentic Brownian landscape.

Records Restorers Dream Of

Is it because so many of us drive through Croome Park without knowing it that Croome counts as a Hidden Garden? Partly. Croome has also been overlooked by many garden historians: if it appears at all in books on the period, it tends to get a mere passing mention as one of Brown's early designs before the author goes on to more meaty matters.

It turns out that the English word 'garden' is an elastic term, and the Croome project stretches it to its limits. At Croome it is expected to encompass a vast acreage of park and landscape.

The estate map drawn by John Snape in 1796 shows Brown's design as it matured. The National Trust is restoring the remaining garden to around this date. At bottom left is a sketch of Dunstall Castle, the 'ruin' Robert Adam designed for Lord Coventry for a vista from your house'.

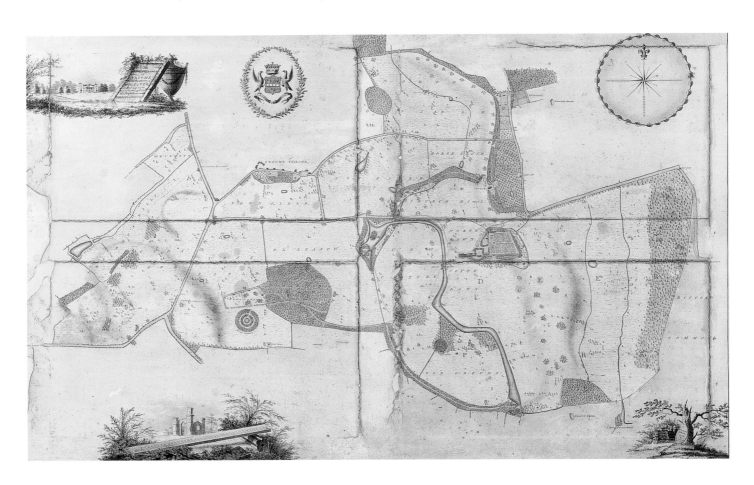

A Hidden Gardens criterion is also the fact that the landscape is undergoing 'restoration' in the best garden history sense (as defined by Sylvia Landsberg, see page 23): 'sufficient remains have survived to enable the garden to be returned to its former glory'. Croome also excels in the 'reconstruction' department, with abundant documentary evidence to complement the physical remains on the ground. The Croome Estate Trustees have superb, largely untapped archives. The estate records for Croome turn out to be among the most complete of any historic landscape and there are three fine estate maps from 1763, 1796 and 1810. The information they contain is so accurate that GPS positioning and geophysics confirm the routes of paths, areas of planting and even the position of individual trees. There is also an unimagined wealth of letters and papers, bills and plant lists.

Contemporary comments written by visitors naturally call for a pinch of salt, but confirm that the effect was impressive. Some are quoted by William Dean, the head gardener, who wrote a guide book to Croome as the plantings came of age in 1824. This slim volume is valuable on several levels – aside from its vitally important plant list, the 'Hortus Croomensis', of which more later. You might expect Dean's tone of fulsome praise and sentences of Proustian length to make it dismissable as a period piece rather than an objective description. (The Worcester typesetters were not short of a comma or two.) It is useful, however, partly as an account by someone who knew the site inside out, and partly because it conveys vividly the vision that the visitor was expected to share. Or the visions, plural, because this was essentially a landscape to be discovered from a series of different viewpoints as you moved through it. Mr Dean (aided by an anonymous friend) engagingly personified his reader: 'In the course of a walk through it, it is proposed to point out to the stranger, some of the principal objects, worthy of notice.' We – readers, viewers, visitors – are now invited to step into the shoes of Mr Dean's 'stranger'. We can admire and wonder. But we today also have the benefit of hindsight (and a measure of undercover information) to guide us through the historic landscape.

The Panorama Tower was built as an eyecatcher to stand on Knight's Hill, Cubsmoor, at the western extremity of the park. James Wyatt based the design on Adam's ideas. Today it lies outside the Croome Park estate, to the west of the M5, and still acts as an eyecatcher.

The Grave Young Lord
and the Capable Young Brown

The young lord George William was grave (in Horace Walpole's description) because in unexpectedly inheriting his title he had lost his closest friend – his brother Thomas, Lord Deerhurst, just one year older, with whom he had studied at Winchester and Oxford, and with whom he planned a career in politics. Out of the blue Thomas died in 1744 at the age of 23. Catherine Gordon, in her splendid account of Croome, attributes the single-mindedness with which the sixth earl threw himself into improving the family estate in some part to 'an overwhelming sense of duty, a passionate desire to fulfil the expectations of his brother, and compensate for his own sense of unworthiness and inadequacy'. George William was also a highly cultured individual in the happy position of possessing a large fortune commensurate to his tastes.

The estate was settled on George William, the new Viscount Deerhurst, in 1748, and he then inherited the earldom when his father, the fifth earl, died in 1751. Croome Park, to which he now turned his attention, was not entirely a blank canvas. It was already the largest estate in Worcestershire when his father, William Coventry, had inherited in 1719, somewhat against the odds. (The line of inheritance took unexpected twists in the years before his turn came: Nash, the county historian, claimed that 'nearly forty persons died, any one of whom would have inherited before him'.) The fifth earl rose to the task. He embarked upon a sequence of modest improvements, almost doubling the annual rental income in fifteen years. Astute land management was the order of the day, and the earl did what his peers were doing. Trees were planted, land drained and new farm buildings constructed. Parcels of land were exchanged to consolidate the area of parkland around the house, and other land was enclosed into fields.

George William continued this process after his brother's death in 1744, gradually formulating grander and more ambitious ideas. Again,

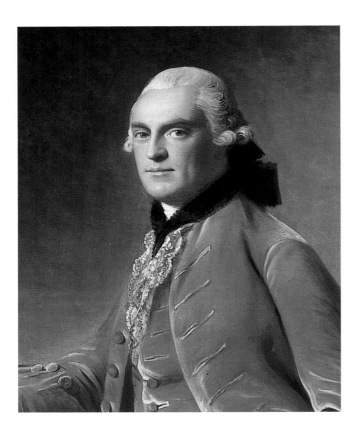

George William Coventry (1722–1809) became sixth Earl of Coventry in 1751. A man of taste and culture, his wealth from agricultural 'improvements' enabled him to patronize many of the most distinguished artists and craftsmen of the day. He was painted by Allan Ramsay in c1765.

the economic tide was in his favour. The number of leaseholders was neatly reduced between 1749 and 1750 by doubling the rent. With the help of one John Phipps, George William began to take stylistic steps in parallel: as his friend Sanderson Miller wrote, his 'Lordship's spirit of improvement begins to exert itself'. The formal gardens around the house were swept away – by John Phipps, before 'Capability' Brown appeared. New hothouses were built and pineapples planted. An artificial river was completed by 1748, describing a simple curve round to the south-west of the house and terminating in a grove of trees. William Halfpenny built a Chinese bridge over the 'river'. A survey made by John Doherty in about 1751 shows these improvements to be a hotchpotch, lacking cohesion. Capable help was at hand.

The catalyst was George William's gentleman-architect friend Sanderson Miller, who visited Stowe, where Lancelot 'Capability' Brown was head gardener, in November 1749. He was shown around by Brown, whom he invited to his estate at Radway in Warwickshire the following summer. Here, it seems, Brown was introduced to the new Lord Deerhurst. Something clicked between them. By 1751 Lancelot 'Capability' Brown was designing a new Palladian exterior to the house at Croome Court for Deerhurst, now Lord Coventry. His brief rapidly grew to encompass the wider landscape.

Brown worked intermittently for Lord Coventry between 1751 and his death in 1782. There were two concentrated periods during 1751–6 and 1762–6. Brown remodelled the Jacobean house using Bath stone and built the offices, stables and church. Part of the house interior and the church interior were entrusted to Robert Adam, who worked at Croome from 1760 and again around 1779. In the park Brown did initial designs for the Rotunda, Sabrina's Grotto, the Dry Arch, the Island Temple and the wooden bridges in the garden (though most of these were altered later). Robert Adam designed most of the important buildings in the park – the Temple Greenhouse, the Alcove or Park Seat, the London Arch and the Pier Gates. James Wyatt completed some of this work

Lancelot 'Capability' Brown (1715–1783), painted by Nathaniel Dance in about 1770. Croome Park was a landmark in Brown's early career, and he continued to be involved in its development into the 1760s. By the time of this portrait Brown's relationship with Lord Coventry was one of friendship rather than service.

after Adam's death. The catalogue of the other skilled workers Lord Coventry employed at Croome and elsewhere reads like a Who Was Who in top interior design (from Robert Adam to the Venetian painter Antonio Zucchi) of the best part of the eighteenth century.

It's no more possible to encapsulate Capability Brown's career in this small space than to squeeze a shrubbery into a flowerpot. Brown's genius lay in 'seeing' what was not yet there. He could make slight gradients look like soaring slopes, and could enable others to see in that way too. His ability embraced engineering and classical architecture, though the actual construction of his buildings might be done by other hands. Here we concentrate on what Croome must have meant to Brown and vice versa. Two strands predominate, the drainage and the plantings.

The house lay in a shallow bowl, with rising ground to the east. Brown remodelled the terrain and used trees in clumps, belts and shrubberies to make the most of views to and from the house. A new lake was made and the artificial river was enlarged and moulded into its present Severn-like meandering course, with its source in Sabrina's Grotto. One of Brown's triumphs was the installation of a 'back-to-front' ha-ha. The normal ha-ha assures a seamless view from the house with its surrounding mown lawns to the smooth grazed turf of the adjacent parkland. 'Pleasure ground and park continued to be distinct entities – the former maintained by gardeners, the latter by livestock – but the widespread adoption of the ha-ha was bringing them into increasing visual integration, and thus ensured the continued migration of aesthetic features out from the former to the latter' (Tom Williamson, *Polite Landscapes*). For Brown, the views from the park of the house in its setting were as important as those from the house.

One of the most radical, albeit subtle, differences between today's landscape and that of Brown's day is the texture of the sweeping expanses of grass – the 'connecting medium'. William Dean wrote of 'the rich verdure…animated with an abundance of hares and other game, in busy or sportive action; and with flocks and herds, browsing on the grass, or reposing in the shade'. (He specified that the cows were of the Holderness and Alderney breeds.) In recent decades the profit of the land has been derived from cereals, and one of the National Trust's aims is to restore a grazing regime. Dean thought it not 'improper to remark that when the park is thus brought into close contact with the house and the pleasure grounds; and forms the connecting medium, between them and the surrounding country: it should, nearer home, partake of the neatness and elegance of the one; and, at a greater distance, show something of the natural wildness of the other.' Isn't this how natural garden designers are telling us to vary our grass mowing today? '…the great Designer of Croome…has allowed the park scenery, round the house, to take a higher polish – whilst, at a distance, and towards the boundaries, the woods already begin to assume, and, with advancing time will assume, more and

'In carrying his vast plans into effect, it must be owned, the noble improver did not niggardly spare the cost – since, it is said that he has, here, expended no less a sum than four hundred thousand pounds.'

William Dean

more, of the wild grandeur of forest scenery.' The landscape became a model of agricultural and productive efficiency as well as beauty. It also became the acme of state-of-the-art horticultural practice and up-to-date plant interest.

Judicious and Extensive Drains

One of the points stressed by many of the eighteenth-century commentators was the way the landscape had been transformed. A correspondent to the *Gentleman's Magazine* in 1792 was 'charmed, in the highest degree, as to the gratification of my eyes'. Not only had he never seen a more perfect spot, nor any kept in such perfect order, but: 'A vast extent of ground, formerly a mere bog, is now adorned with islands and tufts of trees of every species; and watered around, in the most pleasing, and natural manner, possible.' Mr Darke, in the First Agricultural Survey of 1794, was particularly keen on the drains. 'The most skilful drainer I know…was the late Earl of Coventry. His part of the country was a morass, not more than half a century back: but is now perfectly dry, sound for sheep and other cattle. It may justly be called a pattern farm for the whole kingdom, from its well-formed plantations, and its judicious and extensive drains.'

Hydrologist Nick Haycock explains the logic of Croome's waterworks to Chris Beardshaw. Brown's enduring underground architecture is as important to the site as the classical buildings above ground.

One of the attributes of genius is to make its achievements seem effortless. 'Here is seen a fine expanse of water – which Art has formed, but which Nature might own,' apostrophized William Dean. 'It is a scene of calm delight; the majestic repose of nature; where all is serene and solemn; infusing a deep, enthusiastic, almost awful stillness into the mind, which may be felt but cannot be described.' The surface view still impresses, but what infuses awe into Chris Beardshaw's mind is the extraordinary amount of hidden hydraulic expertise that went into the making of this picturesque perfection.

The person who makes drainage sound positively lyrical is Nick Haycock who is the consultant hydrologist employed by Jamie Whitehouse and his restoration team. We are accustomed to admiring the classical buildings and ornaments that Brown dotted about the landscape – artistically, we might say. But we learn that what is truly admirable are the quality and contours of the limestone watercourses that run out of sight underground. Therein lies his finest Art.

It seems that Lord Coventry wanted a river frontage. He wanted something that looked like the river Severn not far away, meandering in generous serpentine loops. Brown planned a Severn in miniature: a one-fifth-scale version, a mile-and-a-half (2.4km) long, of the course of the river on the boundary of the Croome estate. Brown later became famous for his 'rivers', yet this first one was probably made at the request of Lord Coventry. It was to be a steep learning curve.

The Severn provided the inspiration but also caused a large part of the problem. The ground was naturally a boggy mire, or 'a morass' as Brown's memorial at Croome states in capital letters. Impossible to cultivate for crops, it was grazed by cattle. The landscape was formed by one of the many courses of the Severn charged with glacial meltwaters before it reverted to its current course at the foot of the Malverns some four thousand years ago. Two distinct geologies meet here: heavy, compacted, blue Jurassic clay and the sticky, claggy red clays of the Triassic. They are overlaid by a mosaic of glacial gravel deposits and silt. Although he could read the vegetation as well as any modern ecologist and know that plants like silverweed and horsetail are indicators of damp ground, Brown presumably would not know what kind of substrate he would encounter in any given spot where he sank his spade.

Brown's vision was one of clarity. He wanted a clear, reflective water surface – essentially a classical concept. He also wanted a seamless pastoral landscape sweeping up to the house, so there was no question of visible drains and ditches. Everything had to go underground. He must have begun in the area around the house. Nick Haycock points out a splendid brick-lined culvert almost high enough to walk through near the house. Others are square limestone drains with flagstones on top. 'There's one drain a mile-and-a-half [2.4km] long, and we now know the drop on that is only 6 inches [15cm],' he marvels. 'That's the precision of Roman engineers. It's fantastic engineering.' Brown sometimes dug down 8 feet (2.5m) or so to lay a drain. Nick estimates they used about two-

Before restoration Brown's artificial Croome River – created in the eighteenth century 'where no river ran' – is hidden from sight by rank vegetation and marginal weeds. Capability Brown envisaged a tract of clear water, visible from a distance. Whether the margins were to be kept clear by grazing stock or scything gardeners is unknown.

and-a-half million bricks. The drains were tough, too. Some of the structures began to collapse only in the last ten or fifteen years under the weight of heavy modern farm machinery used at harvest. And all this before he 'really started to carve up the landscape' – grade down the slopes and flatten out the flood plain. It was all tied in to view lines to 'sweeten up' the views from the house. The scale of the effort and the cost seem unthinkable today.

And then – Brown's river didn't work. He was a victim of his own success. He created too effective a drainage system. It collected all the winter water and shot it straight into the lake and river with the result that the site was bone dry in summer, and the water level in the lake became too low. It takes an enormous amount of water – 'We're talking about a whole winter's rainfall to fill it,' says Nick Haycock. Brown was forced to go further and further afield to bring water in to top up the lake.

There was another problem. The varying geology meant that in some places the lake was over impermeable clay, but elsewhere the substrate consisted of loose sands and gravels, and here they had to introduce a puddled clay lining. During the restoration Nick Haycock and his team are discovering a patchwork of different sections. There was always an assumption that Brown would have puddled the whole area with clay to make it watertight. 'But you're talking about 20 acres (8ha) of water – that's a big area to puddle.' The Croome Estate archives show that Lord Coventry was constantly writing letters to Brown saying, 'We're losing water, please come back!'

Paradoxically one of the National Trust's restoration strategies is to restore some of the 'morass' that was so proudly eliminated in the eighteenth century. Ecologists now recognize that the old wetlands were sponges, holding the winter water and releasing it slowly during the summer to keep the flow going. Brown too must have come to realize that you couldn't let all the water flow away into the lake but had to hang on to some of it, and that the land needed a steady supply. His later schemes involved additional reservoirs, extra supplies of water. Chris wonders to what extent the watercourses he made at other sites like Blenheim owe their success to what he learned here in this very

It takes the right viewpoint and the right light to see the 'mirrored water' that Capability Brown had in mind. A handful of the trees, like the cedars reflecting in Croome Lake, date from his time.

difficult site: 'It really did set him up and he did become a kind of water specialist.'

Incidentally excavating the new wetlands is providing material to create a berm or bank between the main park and the motorway, helping to screen out noise and pollution once trees are planted. It's a huge task, involving dozens of bright yellow and orange diggers and dozers, each shifting in a load what Lord Coventry's locals would have taken a day to move. Capability Brown would have been impressed.

Grounds for Pleasure

In common with visitors to Croome, who often have only a couple of hours to 'do' this great garden, we will have to whiz through, pausing at what catches our interest. By the late eighteenth century, when more

The island in the lake at the western end of Brown's river is linked to the 'mainland' by two fine bridges displaying early examples of wrought ironwork. The 'stranger' visiting Croome for the first time is enticed to cross a bridge to inspect Robert Adam's Island Pavilion, with its Coade stone reliefs.

land had been added to the estate, there were two principal circuits: a 3-mile (4.8km) walk and a 10-mile (16km) ride. (We have two-and-a-half centuries to cover, too.) Besides the second Lady Coventry's Menagerie on Cubsmoor (where exotic rare birds vied with architecture by Adam), particular attractions were the Wilderness and the Arboretum, which had more than 300 exotic trees (and where the young botanist might be aided and gratified 'to find the botanical

The Dry Arch (Brown's idea) allowed visitors making the circuit on foot to pass beneath the main carrriageway from the west without interruption and see the lakeside gardens.

The Temple Greenhouse or conservatory made an important feature in the landscape among the trees between the church and the foot of Church Hill. Robert Adam's first park building, designed in 1760 for 15 guineas, it was fitted with large removable sash windows to protect the tender plants that were overwintered inside.

name of every tree painted on sticks, and thrust into the ground, near the roots of each'). A key attraction was the Flower or Botanic Garden, with a rockwork pool, a conservatory for Chinese plants and exotic houses dedicated to plants from the East and West Indies and the Cape. Many of the plants were collected by members of the family and by friends, but a great number were purchased from the burgeoning nursery trade in exotics. By 1801 Arthur Young (*Annals of Agriculture*) rated Croome as second only to Kew botanical garden.

Papers from the 1760s onwards document the acquisition of some of these plants and serve as a gazetteer of plant exploration. William Dean's 'Hortus Croomensis' is the culmination of a growing collection. It lists some 5000 plants grown at Croome in the form of a 140-odd-page catalogue, from *Abroma* (defined as an East Indies Stove shrub) to *Zygophyllum* or Bean Caper from Syria and the Cape of Good Hope (defined as a greenhouse shrub). William Dean or his publisher had an astute eye on the gardening book market. A number of the subscribers to Dean's book were nurserymen, and at the end he included useful advice on propagating some of the novelties, as well as recipes for the best compost mixtures for various new exotics.

The first Lady Coventry, born Maria Gunning (1732–60), was a townie. In 1764 Lord Coventry remarried. Barbara, the daughter of the tenth Baron of St John of Bletsoe, who brought with her a large dowry and an active interest in Croome. In return Lord Coventry promptly gave her the menagerie, and a model farm and model dairy as a source of pin-money. Best of all she was interested in horticulture. She often mentioned seeds and plants in her correspondence with her sister. 'You have made mine the best furnished greenhouse in this country. The seeds from Botany Bay are not yet come. I will send some to you as soon as I have them.' The letter is undated, but Botany Bay appeared on the horticultural map when Captain James Cook returned from his groundbreaking voyage in 1771.

When garden history focuses only on architecture and style, a vital dimension is missing – the plants that vitalize the picture. There should be no danger of this at Croome. The planting bills and lists in the archives track every aspect of the estate, and bring alive the buildings, as when Dean writes of the temple: 'This building being closed up, in front, with glass windows, is used as a greenhouse in winter: and when these are removed, it becomes an agreeable summer apartment.' Nor was garden appreciation all aesthetics and serious admiring of prospects. There were visitors to entertain. The new garden buildings and parkland at Croome made a perfect setting for boating parties, picnics and firework displays. Bills from a firework artist in Holborn itemize Chinese Trees of Silver Flowers, Italian Suns, Roman Candles, Gold Flower-pots and Water Rockets.

But there was serious plantsmanship and plants-oneupmanship too.

What the Plant Lists Tell

You find boatloads of elms being sent upriver from Gloucester in the 1740s and men being paid a penny a day for planting trees. Species might be ordered as seed, mast, acorns, chestnuts (this suggests they must have had vast nursery areas); but sometimes the landowner or his agent are not willing to wait, and order the more expensive seedling trees.

Croome Park's apparently natural beauty was achieved only by means of extensive underground drains, which lasted 250 years until heavy agricultural machinery began to damage them. This is the last of the arable crops: after the 2003 harvest the land is being reseeded as pasture, and additional trees such as oaks will be planted.

When you find orders by the thousand – 2000 two-year-old oaks or 1000 year-old larches, Scotch firs, silver firs, spruce; 2500 beech, birch and mountain ash – you realize there's some serious landscaping going on, bread-and-butter shelter-belt and woodland planting. Orders for 500 Weymouth pine, 250 hornbeam, 100 red cedars and 25 tulip trees show the improver also has quality in mind. Quality invested in trees works both ways: these are not just handsome ornamentals, but harvestable timber too.

Equally functional are occasional orders for box by the yard, probably for the kitchen garden. Utilitarian items like netting, pruning knives, strong nails and vast quantities of mats, for plant protection, appeal to the hands-on gardener. Agriculture is represented by orders for buckwheat, white or Dutch clover, ryegrass, sanfoin, trefoil, and the arcane 'canary' (presumably the grass *Phalaris canariensis*). The kitchen garden is regularly restocked with seed-grown vegetables as well as asparagus plants and seed potatoes (sometimes the 'red-nose kidney' variety) and mushroom spawn is ordered for the mushroom house. There are hardy fruit trees for an orchard or training on the kitchen-garden walls. (Dean recorded that the home shrubbery sheltered 'a 7-acre kitchen garden well stocked with fruit trees; and well furnished with pineries, vineries, and peach houses,' and we duly find vines, pineapples and melons on order.)

But it is the ornamental plants newly imported from a number of distant continents that mark milestones in Britain's horticulture. From the heyday of the transatlantic plant exchange in the 1760s with its kalmias and andromedas, mahonias and maples, you can see items such as sophoras and leptospermums marking the progress of plant

Plants in the Wilderness Walk are restricted to those available in England before 1800, such as *Rosa rubiginosa*.

hunting expeditions like Cook's round the globe; in the early 1790s Lord Coventry was ordering Antipodean plants like metrosideros, banksias, New Zealand flax and Botany Bay lily, Botany Bay fig and Botany Bay jasmine. There were mesembryanthemums and proteas from the Cape, camellias and ginkgo from China and, signalling another new phase in plant introductions, orders for China magnolia and new China roses. 'Hortus Croomensis' helps us know how these plants were treated at Croome – how, a generation later, experience had shown they should be cosseted under shelter or in heated houses, or grown outdoors.

One introduction was not to be a problem at Croome. We find Lord Coventry acquiring *Rhododendron ponticum* in 1791, thirty years after it was introduced to England. In more acidic areas this novelty has become a curse, and the National Trust is at pains to remove its blanketing cover from many thousands of acres.

Novelties and Nurseries

We also glimpse aspects of the socio-horticultural history of the nursery trade, and the development of demand and supply. Like 'useful' forest trees, exotics were obtained from nurserymen and plant collectors

either as plants or as seed. Many exotics were complete novelties. Few plants were resilient enough to survive the Atlantic crossing, packed however carefully in boxes of sand or whatever, so seed, or dormant rhizomes or bulbs, were the common currency. It must have been an adventurous gardener who set about growing these unknown plants, and there was great competition to see who succeeded. Landowners like Lord Coventry, who were hungry for novelty, spurred the demand.

It was the heyday of James Gordon's nursery (to be found at 'the last house on the left at Mile-end' in what is now east London). He was the wizard who succeeded in getting tricky new seeds to sprout. When Croome acquired rhododendrons and acacias from Gordon, as evidenced by the bill of 1 March 1760, the gardeners were advised to 'stick yew or holly round them to preserve them from the bleak winds'. The specimens were precious not just for their novelty value, but because they were so hard to propagate. Gordon was quite exceptional in his success in germinating some of the difficult Ericaceae arriving from America. 'What shews his great knowledge and experience in vegetation is his way of raising the finest dusty seeds,' Peter Collinson commented in admiration. Collinson was the unsung Quaker cloth merchant and haberdasher at the hub of the exchange of plants to and fro across the Atlantic, and also with numerous European contacts. 'Before him, I never knew or heard of any man that could raise the dusty seeds of the Kalmias, Rhododendrons, or Azaleas. These charming, hardy shrubs, that excel all others in his care, he furnishes to every curious garden; all the nurserymen and gardeners come to him for them.'

Collinson also recorded that in 1763, 'after more than 20 years' trial', Gordon showed him 'the Loblolly Bay of Carolina coming up from seed in a way not to be expected; this elegant evergreen shrub is next in beauty to the Magnolia's, and his sagacity in raising all sorts of Plants from cuttings, roots and layers surpasses all others by which our gardens are enriched…' In 1766 we find Lord Coventry receiving one or more specimens of loblolly bay (named *Gordonia lasianthos* in Gordon's honour) from nurseryman Clark along with other American plants like andromedas, rhododendrons, swamp pines (*Taxodium distichum*) and honeysuckles.

With the firms of Stavely & Cross, Powell & Eddie, George Ferne or John Williamson you can correlate what's going to Croome with

The shrubby ornamental blackberry *Rubus odoratus*, also known as thimbleberry, was introduced to Britain from eastern North America in 1770, so fits in perfectly with the era when Croome's first shrubberies were being planted.

Opposite The wealth expended on plants by Lord Coventry is commemorated in the extensive archive material held by the Trustees of the Croombe Estate, such as these bills from Messrs Lee & Kennedy.

Watersides attract hosts of marginal weeds and seedling trees that obscure the clean lines and clear reflections you see idealized in paintings. A certain amount of cover is desirable, but vigilant gardening is necessary to keep this habitat groomed to just the right degree.

what's just arrived from North America via Peter Collinson from John Bartram in Philadelphia. Many improving landowners like the Duke of Richmond subscribed directly to Collinson's system of 'five-guinea boxes', but Lord Coventry preferred to get his novelties through a network of nurserymen who themselves paid their five guineas and in return received something of a lucky-dip boxful of seeds. In June 1760 Peter Collinson informed Bartram of 'what Seed will be wanting next fall', and listed the customers, beginning with '2 five-guinea boxes for Gordon who hath sett up a Seed Shop' and including nurserymen Powell & Eddie, Williamson, Ferne, Webb and Bush – all of whom are supplying Croome with seeds. John Bush has a special place in the Croome story, and the two boxes for John Bush were to be specially marked and were to be filled 'with pines, Firrs, Acorns, Beach, Chesnut and all Other Trees…Catalpa & Alders, Junipers, Cedars,

Maples, Birches, Services, Wallnuts, Hickeries, Planes, Padus Cherry, poplars, Tulip Tree, small Magnolia, Mountain Magnolia, &c.' Nurseryman Bush was specializing in good landscape trees.

John Bush wanted seeds of 'the Large forrest tree kind' for 'his friends in Germany' and in 1764 complained that last year's three boxes of seeds 'proved not to Expectation'. Collinson annotated the letter: 'I dont know what to Do with these Germans...Some of the Boxes was open'd, & plundered, by the Spaniard...one of Gordons I saw was served So, possibly these might be so too.' The challenges of importing seeds included weather and enemies. Coventry received American plants and seeds brought from Philadelphia by Captain Bolitho on the *Myrtilla* in 1759. Collinson had been worried about the state of these cargoes: 'of the Living plants Sent I can give but a poor account...many of them was Stumps without Fibers so I had no hopes of them but Live in Expectation they may shoot' (May 1759).

When garden history focuses on plant lists without acknowledging the challenges contemporary gardeners faced in nurturing these unknown precious cargoes, a further dimension – that of the practical gardener – gets lost. Everyone who tries to grow new things knows that gardening is full of surprises, good and bad. The voice of shared experience can be a lingua franca between people of very different background and degree. Capability Brown, in his later years, visited Croome as a friend rather than an employed professional, and it was after visiting the Coventrys in their London home that he was taken ill and died.

Lord Coventry's acknowledgement of Lancelot 'Capability' Brown's achievement was embodied in a monument placed near Croome Lake with an eloquent inscription.

TO THE MEMORY OF

LAUNCELOT BROWN,

WHO, BY THE POWERS OF HIS INIMITABLE AND CREATIVE GENIUS, FORMED THIS GARDEN SCENE OUT OF

A MORASS.

May it please Your Lordship

I have the Honer to acquaint you that I and family are safe arrived at Petersburg after 9 Days passage from England her Imperial Majesty reced me very graciously & placed me in one of her palaces called Oranienbaum,

I have sent your Lordship a Box of plants mark'd I & C N⁰ 3 Consign'd to Dr Fothergill, p Ship General Conway Capt Robt Lumley, which I hope will come safe I hope we next spring when the plants are in bloom shall find more sorts, it is dangerous in these woods to collect plants there being Large Bears & wolves,

I am Your Lordships
Most Hum & obed Servt

John Bush

Oranienbaum
Sept 26th 1771

the following is the Catalogue

a Sweet scented flower

N⁰
1 Vaccinium
2 a plant Unknown with a
Black Stalk Fern
3 Birch
4 Pyrola
5 Creeping Vaccinium
6 Water palae
7 Geranium
8 Dwarf Bramble
9 Rhododendron 10 plants
10 a Fern
11 a plant Unknown
12 a plant Unknown
13 Lilly de Valle minor
14 Lilly de Valle major
16 Orchis 6 plants

£5 - 5 - 0

please to pay the money to mr Mello N⁰ 36 Fenchurch Street
please To direct for me to the Care of Messrs
Weltden Baxter & Freedrick
at
St Petersburg

A Tale of One Bush

John Bush also acquired something of a special relationship with Lord Coventry and became one of those people for whom gardening and horticulture dissolved class barriers. John Bush or Busch (plantsmen and gardeners so often have appropriate names) offers a slice of international garden history, laced with adventure. Born in Hanover, he moved to London in 1744 and ran a successful nursery in Hackney, which he sold when he received an irresistible invitation to Russia in 1771. (Under its new owner, Conrad Loddiges, the nursery became one of the best-known names in the business.)

On his arrival in Russia John Bush sent Lord Coventry – care of Dr John Fothergill, the celebrated Quaker physician and plantsman – a box of woodland plants, including various unknowns, a black-stalked fern, some rhododendrons and vacciniums, and lily of the valley. The accompanying letter acquainted his lordship that Bush and his family were safely arrived at St Petersburg after nine days' passage from England. He hoped the box would come safely, and that when plants were in flower again next spring he might be able to find more sorts: 'it is dangerous in these woods to collect plants there being large bears and wolves.' The box of plants apparently arrived, but not without incident. Annotation on the letter revealed that the ship – the *General Conway* under Captain Robert Lumley – had foundered on the coast of Scotland. The message, however, seems to have got through.

Bush reported: 'Her Imperial Majesty received me very graciously and placed me in one of her palaces called Oranienbaum.' The lady in question was Catherine the Great and Oranienbaum (Lomonosov) was one of the splendid palaces built under Peter the Great. Bush, preferred over other English landscapers because like Catherine he was German-speaking, went on to create the park with picturesque lakes and pools at Gatchina, the palace of Catherine's favourite, Count Gregory Orlov. With the Russian architect Vasily Neyelov he also created the famous park to the south and west of the Ekaterininsky palace at Tsarskoe Selo (renamed Pushkin in the 1930s). They reformed the formal pool into a large lake with promontories and inlets, altered the contours to create other stretches of water, and planted trees. Architectural features included those that were classically inspired (Neyelov's Palladian bridge took after that at Wilton House in

John Bush wrote to Lord Coventry to report his family's safe arrival in St Petersburg. The tone of his letter is as much one of friendship as that of a supplier of plants.

Wiltshire), or built in Turkish or Chinese style. The Ekaterininsky Park is one of the earliest examples of landscaping in the English style in Russia. English influence had been taken east by a German.

There were echoes of Croome and Brown's other landscapes in Catherine's domain. She told Voltaire in 1772 how she scorned straight lines and formality: 'I now love to distraction gardens in the English style…the curving lines, the gentle slopes, the ponds in the form of lakes, the archipelagoes on dry land…in a word, anglomania rules my plantomania.' English landscape parks adorned the 950-piece table service Catherine ordered from Wedgwood and Bentley, and English (and Scottish) architects designed many of the structures in her gardens.

Utility and Beauty

Once the literally ground-breaking restoration scheme currently being implemented by the National Trust is completed and begins to mature, Croome Park will again become more like the scenes painted on Catherine's dinner service. But the days when a landowner or a sovereign could call the tune are long gone. Some 200 years before the M5 was built, the man who commissioned Brown to create the park allowed strategic turnpike roads to pass over his lands and welcomed the better-sprung coaches that enabled both passengers and post to travel between Croome Park and London in under two days. Today the journey can take under two hours. However, George William, sixth Earl of Coventry, would never have countenanced a mere public road to mar the grand design of his Croome parkland. He took pains to shield the surroundings of Croome Court from such troublesome thoroughfares and he rerouted the public road from Pershore to the Severn so that it ran to the north side of Croome church, further from the Court. Later he improved the quality of other access routes around the village of Severn Stoke. Long after his day, railway technology replaced the Severn and its canal network as the main freight route.

Today, as vapour trails lace the sky and motorway white noise clouds the air, the sort of time capsule offered by spaces like Croome Park becomes increasingly precious. All the more important that they are restored to life and revitalized with the promise of a living future. They are our national treasure. They belong to our National Trust. This land is our land.

Capability Brown resited the Church of St Mary Magdalene on the brow of a hill to the north of Croome Court. It is now maintained by the Churches Conservation Trust, but it still serves as an eyecatcher in the landscape.

BRIDGE END GARDEN

An Intimate and Even Secret Place

Vandals despoiled Rome of its art and its treasures in 455. Today vandalism is a byword for wanton damage – particularly, in recent generations, in public spaces like parks. Bridge End Garden has had its share. Over the twentieth century several of the fine works of art and architectural pieces lovingly assembled by Francis Gibson were damaged, or disappeared. A fine seventeenth-century lead Triton attributed to Jan Van Nost had to be removed for safe keeping. Even in today's climate of care and security cameras, occasional graffiti and empty vodka bottles appear. Bad behaviour, it seems, is not new. The fact that a notice of Garden Regulations needed to be posted way back in 1919 suggests that even park keepers, respect and respectability were not proof against wanton damage. 'No Writing, Figures, or Marks shall be placed or inscribed on any Tree, Wall, Fence, Building, Seat, or other Property in the Gardens,' went one rule; another declared: 'No person shall cut, pluck, or injure any Tree, Bush or Flower.'

So to cut down some thirty soaring yew trees in Bridge End Garden is an injury some garden lovers can't forgive or forget. Vandalism, some would call it, yet it was done in the name of restoration and historical accuracy. The yews had been planted as topiary specimens but after many decades of neglect had outgrown their intended shapes. To restore the original proportions, the trees were dramatically coppiced or cut back.

Here is a major dilemma. Restoration can be comedy or tragedy according to point of view. People become attached to the atmosphere and romance of a garden in a run-down state. A new restoration, like a new garden, can be horribly raw at first. The restorers can promise regeneration and renewal, but meanwhile for some observers something extraordinary has been lost.

The restorers will assert that the original garden had already been lost when it was allowed to become overgrown and misshapen. Consider the story of the apocryphal observer who remarked, after watching a sculptor carve a stone figure, 'How did you know that man

An Outline of the Plot

You will find Bridge End Garden tucked into a fold of land on the very edge of Saffron Walden, in Essex, between the northernmost streets of houses and open ground variously occupied by playing fields and allotments, then farmland. Gardens were apparently first made here around the start of the nineteenth century by Atkinson Francis Gibson, a local Quaker businessman, but it was under the ownership of his youngest son, Francis Gibson (1805–58), that the fine complex of layouts acclaimed by commentators in the early 1900s appeared. Unusually, these gardens were never attached to a house: Bridge End, the Gibsons' 'homestall' or house and business premises was nearby but separate.

The garden was maintained as a memorial to Francis Gibson after his early death. The Saffron Walden Horticultural Society held its summer fête there intermittently in the nineteenth century. By 1902 Lewis Fry of Bristol, who had married Francis Gibson's daughter, had 'generously thrown [the garden] open to the public as a pleasure ground.' In 1918 Lewis Fry was leasing the garden to Saffron Walden Borough Council at one guinea per annum for local people to enjoy. Today, the artist Anthony (Tony) Fry, owner and one of the garden's trustees, leases the site to Uttlesford District Council.

The second half of the twentieth century was tough on large ornamental gardens. By the 1970s parts of Bridge End Garden had become severely overgrown and the buildings and ornaments vandalized, neglected or lost. The tide began to turn as local concern prompted action and in 1999 a new phase began, with a landscape survey and restoration management plan. In 2001 an application to the Heritage Lottery Fund was successful. The challenge has been to weigh up what evidence can be found and to decide what is authentic in this context. Among the host of early Victorian remains, the main focus of attention from Chris Beardshaw and his TV crew has been the restoration of the Dutch Garden and the adjacent Wilderness.

The shadow of the Eagle Gates at the entrance to the Dutch Garden.

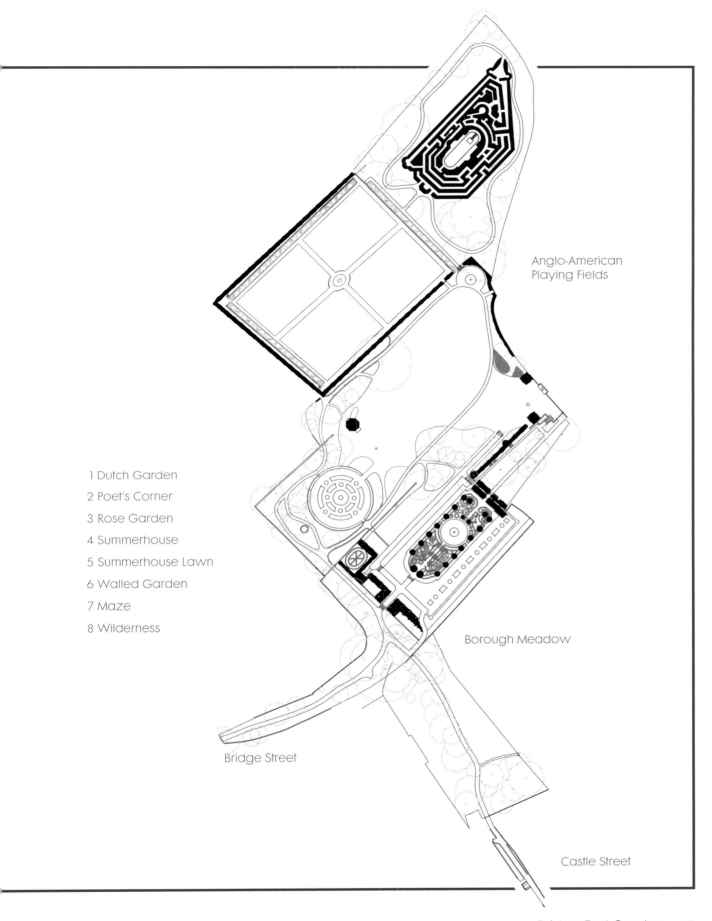

1 Dutch Garden
2 Poet's Corner
3 Rose Garden
4 Summerhouse
5 Summerhouse Lawn
6 Walled Garden
7 Maze
8 Wilderness

Anglo-American
Playing Fields

Borough Meadow

Bridge Street

Castle Street

was hidden in that rock?' At Bridge End people are already beginning to say, 'Good heavens! We had no idea that a garden was hidden amongst those trees!' The debate will continue, as long as gardens grow.

A Hybrid of the Garden Kind

Bridge End Garden defies pigeonholing. It's a private garden, open to the public – emphatically not a public park – and yet because it qualifies as a park, its restoration has been awarded Lottery funding. A garden that is much loved and visited, yet unknown to many on its doorstep.

A garden that inspires great community spirit, yet is sometimes vandalized. A town garden on the edge of town.

Its contours and features are familiar to the people who use it every day as a short cut or as a regular exercise route. It's an escape valve for people seeking a moment of seclusion or a sunny place to sit. Other locals have joined in and become gardeners. All of this proves the thesis of Stewart Harding, director of the Parks Agency, a not-for-profit company, who has been in the forefront of the movement to repair, restore and improve parks and gardens since the 1980s, and who acts as Heritage Lottery Fund monitor for Bridge End Garden. Just as gardens are considered to be good for people, a subset, the urban park, is thought to be good for society. We're talking here of the sort of parks nineteenth-century philanthropists and town planners (like Thomas Mawson see page 146) created, rather than the landscape parks of wealthy landowners like Lord Coventry's at Croome. These are parks for people rather than for deer, game and profit. And to this extent, although Bridge End is not a park, it serves people of the local community and provides that indefinable sense of place. Local people feel at home here and some get involved.

To the newcomer Bridge End Garden comes as a delightful surprise. It is not only alleged 'hidden gardens' that need to be discovered. All gardens have secrets that yield only to the visitor. Your homework may tell you that a garden has 'rooms', like Hidcote, or architectural eye-catchers, like Croome; but until you explore a place yourself you have no idea of the spatial relationships, the excitement of passing from one area to another and discovering, through relative motion, surprise elements in the setting, like the church spire on the horizon.

BOROUGH OF SAFFRON WALDEN.

BRIDGE END GARDENS

These Gardens, which are the Property of The Right Hon. Lewis Fry and temporarily placed by him under the control of the Corporation, are open daily (except when closed by Order of the Corporation) for the use of the Public from 9 a.m. until half-an-hour before Sunset, subject to the following Rules:—

1. No person shall cut, pluck, or injure any Tree, Bush or Flower.
2. No Perambulator, Carriage, or other Vehicle shall be taken into the Gardens.
3. No Bill, Placard, or Notice shall be placed on any Fence, Erection, Building, or Tree in the Gardens.
4. No Writing, Figures, or Marks shall be placed or inscribed on any Tree, Wall, Fence, Building, Seat, or other Property in the Gardens.
5. Climbing of Trees is forbidden.
6. No Public Meetings shall be held or Addresses given in the Gardens without the consent of the Corporation.
7. Dogs are not admitted.
8. Shouting or other annoyances to Visitors prohibited.

NOTE. A Bell will be rung 10 minutes before Closing. Visitors are invited to co-operate with the Custodian in preserving Order.

BY ORDER.

W. ADAMS,
TOWN CLERK.

Saffron Walden.
20th May, 1919.

W. THOMPSON, PRINTER, MARKET PLACE, SAFFRON WALDEN.

49

Fig. 56 Garden Regulations 1919.

Misbehaviour by the public is not a recent phenomenon. The Saffron Walden town clerk drew up this set of regulations for garden visitors in 1919.

Bridge End is a series of complex spaces and this view downhill from Borough Meadow is about as panoramic as possible. The brick wall in the foreground serves as a ha-ha, with the Dutch Garden occupying the level panel of ground beyond. Walls and exotic trees mask the layout of the rising ground, with the summerhouse signalling something worth exploring.

Barely a generation after William Dean wrote his guidebook to Croome Park (see page 41), how would the 'stranger' he addressed as his imagined visitor have found the newly established Bridge End Garden? Would he have been given a guided route and told where to stand and what to enjoy? Or would he have been allowed to discover for himself a layout far more domestic than Croome Park, yet one lacking a house; a design intended to be an intimate and private refuge, yet one beautifully balanced and paced, with measured vistas between elegant structures and intimate enclosures?

'It is a private garden, open to the public, not a municipal park and it is in this spirit that my father wanted it to be enjoyed.'

Tony Fry

Bridge End is unusual in being a houseless garden. Recalling that *focus* in Latin means hearth, you might expect a garden without a house to be like a room without a fireplace, lacking a focal point, lacking warmth. Traditional gardens evolved around a house – Croome Park and

Boveridge are examples of garden and house in inseparable design. Bridge End Garden, however, never had a house at its focus and yet its maker laid it out with its own internal logic and balance.

Bridge End is a garden on the doorstep of the Victorian age, poised on the very edge of Victorian gardening extravagance; opulent, but retaining the chasteness and fastidiousness of its Quaker creator. It was made in a relatively short period of time, but has been remarkably unaltered. It is an extraordinary survival. The restoration team must proceed by attempting to see the place through Francis Gibson's eyes.

Francis Gibson: Banker, Brewer, Artist, Gardener

Francis Gibson was born into a prosperous family. His mother Elizabeth Wyatt was the daughter of a prominent Saffron Walden brewer, and in the 1820s the Gibsons entered banking. His two older brothers immersed themselves in the family businesses. Francis too

Francis Gibson in studious pose in an undated portrait. His diaries reveal him to have been sensitive, conscientious and highly artistic. The maker of Bridge End Garden died aged only 53.

Francis Gibson in studious pose in an undated portrait. His diaries reveal him to have been sensitive, conscientious and highly artistic. The maker of Bridge End Garden died aged only 53.

worked in the bank, and maintained an important presence in local affairs, particularly philanthropic concerns like the regulation of the local poor house. He married Elizabeth Pease of Darlington, youngest daughter of Edward Pease, the Quaker 'father of the Stockton and Darlington Railways'. He fell in love with the North of England and built a house with a manicured garden at Balder Grange in County Durham to visit in the summer months.

In spite of his efficiency in business activity, his real interest seems to have been elsewhere. He had a refined aesthetic sense. He observed and drew and collected, and developed both a keen eye for what he wanted around him in his home and in his garden and a collection of sculptures and paintings. To learn that Gibson, a Quaker, was also a connoisseur comes as a surprise to some of us. Chris Beardshaw quizzes Francis Gibson's great-grandson Tony Fry about the garden aspect of this apparent acquisitiveness, this 'conspicuous consumption'. Tony feels some sympathy as well as kinship with Francis Gibson. He senses that – like many of us – Gibson created his garden to make a place where he could find peace and contemplation.

There's an old saying to the effect that the Quakers' business interests compelled them to make money and their faith compelled them to give it away. Some Quakers could not help becoming wealthy and successful. As with the Huguenots, a Protestant individualism fostered by initial exclusion from the established professions turned Quakers into enterprising tradesmen, craftsmen and businessmen. They also developed a scrupulous sense of taste. In the mid eighteenth century Pehr Kalm, the Swedish botanist, commented on a Quaker community he visited in North America. He noted that although they claimed to scorn fashion 'or to wear cuffs and be dressed as gaily as the others, they strangely enough have their garments made of the finest and costliest material that can be procured'. Neighbouring expatriates from England regarded them as 'semi-Epicureans; for no people want such choice and well-prepared food as the Quakers'. The fact is that Quakers were discerning about quality and discriminating as to how they spent their time and their money.

Francis Gibson's conscientious approach to life is summed up in a diary entry for September 1834:

Order of subjects of Thought and Attention:

1. Religious Duties

2. Domestic Duties

3. Business Duties/Public Duties.

A fourth category would no doubt have been attending to the planning and planting of his Bridge End garden.

One of Francis Gibson's book-plates with its stork emblem is a reminder of his role as intellectual and bibliophile. In 1834 he prepared a lecture on the history of architectural styles, and a similar project on garden styles planned in 1837 may have prompted the new developments in his own Bridge End Garden.

'Following after Gardnering'

The Quakers – like Adam – were born to be gardeners. What would George Fox have thought of the later flowering of his teaching? The founder of the Society of Friends had ordained that schools should teach children 'the nature of herbs, roots, plants and trees'. Early Friends were permitted to 'follow after gardnering' but were expected to plant their gardens 'in a lowly mind and keep to plainness and the serviceable part'. In the late seventeenth and early eighteenth centuries, this would have meant no 'greens' clipped into animal or geometric shapes, so no topiary; no fancy parterres, and no collecting of the unusual flower forms fancied by florists' societies. Probably no stoves for growing tender plants and no greenhouses either.

However, the seeds of gardening that Fox had planted blossomed into an ungovernable passion. By the middle of the eighteenth century the Quakers were celebrated for producing a quite disproportionate number of botanists, nurserymen and plant collectors. That early exclusion from key professions and the universities, and their inclination towards plants and the natural world, encouraged growing expertise in this field. Botanists often developed into apothecaries and physicians, like the connections of Samuel Curtis who created La Chaire (see page 91). Several of the agents who supplied plants to Croome Park were Quakers, and the successful Quaker physician Dr John Fothergill 'procured from all parts of the world a great number of the rarest plants, and protected them in the amplest buildings which this or any country has seen' in his garden at Upton in Essex, according to Sir Joseph Banks. A keen and wealthy gardener, Quaker or not, would keep up with the latest innovations in heated glasshouses in order to be able to grow the latest new plants. Any growing under glass by Francis Gibson seems to have been confined to the kitchen garden and the 'serviceable part', but in designing his pleasure grounds he cannot be described as 'keeping to plainness'. He showed exquisite taste.

> 'Mr Gibson was clearly a man of unusually acute perceptions. At a time when garden design had sunk to a deplorably low ebb, he had the good judgement to fall upon the old traditions, and the dignified effect of the scheme…is proof enough of a considerable power of design.'
>
> *Country Life*
> January 1913

Chris Beardshaw asks Francis Gibson's great-grandson Tony Fry whether the Bridge End Garden seems to square with his Quaker religion. We associate the Quakers with something rather puritanical and austere. Aren't the gardens at Bridge End rather ostentatious? Isn't the Dutch Garden, in particular, somewhat showy – manicured and artificial rather than simple and 'natural'?

We must try to see these things in context, explains Tony Fry, who

has read Gibson's diaries and knows his turn of mind. The gardens at Bridge End are modest in comparison with other gardens that were being laid out in the early half of the nineteenth century. They're not vast, egotistical exploitations of vistas and landscapes. They consist of a series of intimate features in an integrated design – you could almost call them confections – in which we can picture Francis Gibson finding peace for wonder and contemplation, for the inner life that preoccupied him. It seems easy to imagine Francis Gibson seated in the summer-house with his thoughts. We should perhaps see the other areas of his garden in a similar way, as peaceful, orderly places where his eye and mind could wander at will. Today we might even interpret the patterns of the Dutch Garden and the puzzles of the Maze as a sort of mandala, an aid to inner thought.

Summerhouse and cedar: two striking historic features. The summerhouse windows have only recently been replaced, allowing it to serve its intended dual function as focal point and viewpoint. An inscription on the interior is a memorial to Francis Gibson from his widow.

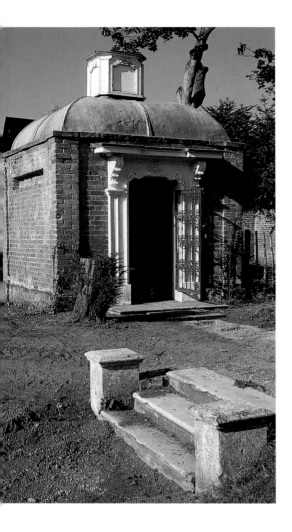

Recently cleared of vegetation, the Pavilion sits between the Dutch Garden and the little Poet's Corner.

There *is* perhaps a Quaker connection, or at least one that involves a religious attitude. While his contemporaries often made the Grand Tour to southern Europe and the Mediterranean, Francis Gibson chose to visit the Protestant Low Countries. He loved Dutch painting, especially the quiet interiors that convey a sense of inner peace. Tony Fry senses that he would have been uncomfortable with the gaudier art of Renaissance Italy and the Catholic world of painters like Raphael. Perhaps this is the clue to his creation of a Dutch garden at a time when it was a novel idea. He even seems to have made its centrepiece that epitome of Dutchness, a piece of leadwork attributed to its supreme master Jan Van Nost.

Dating Dilemmas

Garden restoration always begins with trying to trace just what was where and when on site, as a basis for decisions about what to reinstate. Any clues discovered are set against historic context such as garden fashion. Apparently accurate sources like maps and date plaques can be helpful to garden detectives, but we have to be aware of possible pitfalls. It is not at all clear how much of the Bridge End garden was in existence before it came to Francis in 1829, or when the earliest features were created. The estate he inherited included the homestall (the buildings due north of the Bridge Street path), whatever garden already existed and some 50 acres (20ha) of the surrounding fields. Information from maps is incomplete, but a draft map of the town compiled no later than 1829 shows a hexagonal structure on the spot where the (octagonal) summerhouse stands. It also shows a wall, whose footings were confirmed by archaeology in the 1980s. This is one of the limitations of maps: if their purpose was merely to show a particular aspect of an area – such as information for Poor Rate assessment – to comb them for garden features may be pointless and misleading. The presence of something like the summerhouse may be helpful, but the absence of a feature does not mean it was not there.

A couple of diary entries make oblique allusions. On 19 March 1836 Francis Gibson walked in his garden 'and felt all the reviving and awakening influence of the season'. A few weeks later he mentioned 'the summerhouse, my old…cigar smoking and day dreaming seat' – indicating a familiarity that could date to well before 1829, and the

Gibson's original Coade stone frieze of the Borghese Dancers decorated a parapet where the Summerhouse Lawn gives way to the Wilderness; this is a replica.

first appearance of the summerhouse on an existing map. We don't know how old young Francis was when he began cigar smoking, but daydreaming is a frequent pastime of adolescent aesthetes. We presume that the summerhouse was an early creation, perhaps even predating Francis's inheritance.

Date plaques would seem to be a positive asset. Not always. The date plaques dotted around the Bridge End garden may not be in their original position. One engraved 'G 1814' in one of the Rose Garden walls perhaps represents the date when some part of the garden was begun, but sits oddly in its site and may have been moved there. A Coade keystone in an arch between the Rose Garden and Dutch Garden is also enigmatic. The date 1794 stamped beneath represents the year of manufacture. The brickwork shows that the arch was cut into a previously existing wall. Perhaps only the date on the entrance to the Maze and the date plaque in the Walled Garden are reliable, as we shall see.

Or was the whole design attributable to one William Chater? If you believe the printed word, the assertion in his *Gardeners' Chronicle* obituary looks cut and dried: 'The pretty gardens and grounds at Bridge End, Saffron Walden, were entirely designed and laid out by William Chater, and not a few other places in the county.' William Chater's father was the head gardener at Bower Hall, Steeple Bumpstead, Essex. William (1802–85) set up as a nurseryman and florist in Saffron Walden in 1824 and became famous for breeding hollyhocks. He and Francis Gibson were acquaintances. Both were committee members of the local horticultural

A Coade keystone between the Rose Garden and the Dutch Garden bears the date 1794.

A rose garden should be the epitome of peace and beauty. The Rose Garden at Bridge End had reached a state of real dilapidation by the 1980s, when a rescue plan was launched. The iron hoops supporting climbing roses were repaired, and replacement old varieties planted. The next job is to repair and replace the Archer statue that once stood at its centre.

society, and Gibson's diary for 1834 merely notes in passing that he was 'a respectable and conscientious man'.

The ensemble of Bridge End Garden seems far too idiosyncratic to be anything but the composition of an individual like Francis Gibson. It reveals his hand in its selection of architectural elements and in the sheer whimsicality of some of its components, like the Maze. Perhaps the truth is a compromise, and William Chater helped him lay out certain areas.

Places for Puzzlement and Peace

Before the restoration of the Dutch Garden and the Wilderness, the challenge of returning Francis Gibson's complex creation to something approximating the original – or, at least, of respecting the history of the site while achieving what is practicable – resulted in an interesting series of 'case histories' that display different aspects of restoration strategy.

The Maze was the first project to be tackled by Uttlesford District Council, in 1982. As it matures it may offer some consolation to garden friends discomfited by the brutality of the initial stages of recovering an overgrown garden – the hatchet and chainsaw 'attack' on loved trees. We can date the genesis of the Maze to around 1837, when Francis Gibson noted 'Hampton Court and its Labyrinth' in his 'Memo for London'. It was his custom to collect inspiration as well as artefacts as he travelled about, and his notebooks are full of charming sketches. Within a couple of years the idea had become reality, as a number of pieces of evidence attest. The brick gate piers at the entrance to the Maze bear the roughly engraved inscription 'FEG 1840' – possibly a childish attempt by Gibson's nine-year-old son Francis Edward to imitate the commemorative plaques his father liked to position around the garden. The evidence of dated plaques is not always reliable: they can be moved, or falsified. Here the plants themselves endorse the dating. When the Maze was being restored the original yews were felled and ring-dated. Their unusually clean and uncomplicated trunks revealed that the trees were seedlings in 1835/6 and were transplanted to form the Maze hedges in 1838/9. Further confirmation came from fragments of tesserae excavated from the site of a pavilion of unknown design that was built in the northern part of the Maze. These floor tiles proved to be of a type manufactured by Minton between 1841 and 1846. Twenty years have proved the success of this restoration. The yew hedges have grown tall and make a real puzzle for the 'stranger'. It is not a place to be entered by those in a hurry or with a train to catch.

The Walled Garden demonstrates another standard 'restoration' ploy. As in the Walled Garden at Norton Priory, its current treatment makes absolutely no claim to period authenticity. With the three main walls stabilized and rebuilt where necessary, today the original cruci-form layout of paths with a central pool and statue frames a hybrid garden compartment combining amenity use and working gardening space. From the seat you can enjoy ornamental planting. A compost heap in a corner framed by straw bales is a reminder to visitors of the business of gardening with its message of recycling. It gains points in the purist garden restoration debate by its impermanence: the theory is that just in case full reinstatement of an earlier stage of a garden should ever become feasible, as much as possible of the original should remain. Old kitchen gardens present a particular set of restoration dilemmas. With neither the manpower nor the need to be productive, they need an imaginative identity that does not destroy historical evidence or preclude potential restoration. Yet kitchen garden technology evolved

Francis Gibson's diary for 1837 noted views of London and 'Hampton Court and its Labyrinth'. His Italianate maze at Bridge End was planted in precisely 1839, a date confirmed by tree rings and archaeological evidence when the Maze was replanted and restored in the early 1980s. Contemporary litter included quantities of undated Victorian oyster shells and wine bottles.

Above Francis Gibson's wall
plaque dating the garden
seems indisputable.

Right The Walled Garden on the
high ground at the north-west
edge of the Garden is now laid
out as an ornamental area
around the original central pool.
Beyond the hedge that encloses
its far side, the ground dips
beyond the cedar to the valley
of the Madgate Slade before
rising again to the town, with
St Mary's church spire on
the horizon.

The doorway leading from the Walled Garden to the Maze is surmounted by an elaborate stone arch with a plinth that must surely once have supported a statue.

quite as rapidly as modern kitchens do, and to freeze-frame a particular date would be to take restoration to improbable lengths. Practical gardeners over two centuries have been updating their structures and systems piecemeal and then at intervals throwing the whole lot out and starting again. Few gardens have the funding, the labour supply or the demand for produce to face the decision to revert to Year 'X' and re-create the *status quo*. At Bridge End Garden, for example, the fullest records date from 1918 and list a whole caboodle of peach house, tomato house, cold frames, back-sheds and beehive stands; but this was two generations after Francis Gibson died. The present state seems a satisfactory compromise.

Wilderness, and Paradise Enow

The Summerhouse Lawn and the Rose Garden are on the south-facing slope, and the visitor is inevitably lured down to the gardens in the valley bottom. The lie of the land is shaped by a stream with the Dickensian name of Madgate Slade. Its madness is intermittent. It's a fitful, inconstant watercourse, drying up completely in rainless periods and becoming a rushing torrent when in spate. Given management, it might have fulfilled the role commended by the *Villa Garden Directory* in 1814: 'If a rill pass through the grounds, by adorning its sides with a few groups of shrubbery, and conducting a walk gracefully along the banks, it might be made a source of much pleasure.' Francis Gibson (or perhaps William Chater) did indeed conduct a walk upstream alongside the Madgate Slade towards Ivy Cottage. The views back downhill from here run over the lower ground and up again towards the trees screening the town to terminate in picturesque fashion in the spire of St Mary's on the south-east horizon.

Perhaps because it did not make a satisfactory rill, Gibson sank the stream into a culvert. It is a measure of power, perhaps, or perversity, that landowners (and maybe all gardeners) want to change what they've got. Lord Coventry wanted a river 'where none ran before' and called in Capability Brown. Francis Gibson had a watercourse but chose to hide it. What he did at Bridge End was create a sunken garden over the stream, with a central fountain – fed from elsewhere – as a water feature.

The sunken garden is part of the Dutch Garden which lies at the heart of Bridge End Garden. With the Wilderness, it's the early focus of the current restoration. It was certainly the feature that caught the eye of turn-of-the-century commentators. To the 'stranger' visiting in its heyday, the juxtaposition of the Dutch Garden and the Wilderness must have made a brilliant piece of composition because of the element of contrast – a lost aspect that is now gradually being recovered. A Dutch garden, like a traditional parterre, offers primarily a visual reward. It is designed to be appreciated as a low, open pattern, preferably as a whole, and from above – such as from the upstairs rooms of a house. Bridge End has a cast- and wrought-iron viewing platform to provide the necessary height. The pattern's evergreen outlining means that it is decorative all through the seasons. Seasonal colour effects when bedding plants are renewed are the equivalent of laying a new carpet or changing the sheets, reminding us of Francis Bacon's dismissal of the 'colour-filled knots' of Shakespeare's time as 'but toys; you may see as good sights many times in tarts'. You don't recommend a Dutch garden for plant interest, a function offered by herbaceous borders along the perimeters. Some of the bedding plants might just provide scent as well as colour; but in some Dutch gardens – if you share Queen Anne's nose – you might be equally put off by the cat's-pee smell of box.

A 'wilderness' area offers instead a completely different sensory experience. You are not outside the pattern, admiring its symmetry with your eye, but enclosed and enfolded within a world of plants. Essentially it creates cool shade as an alternative to open daylight. Plants in a wilderness may be structured and repeated, but they are chosen to be admired for themselves – for leaf form, flower and berry colour, scent and habit. Rather than following its visual complexities from a set vantage point, you need to move through it, open to its effects on your senses. The plants are alive as leaves move and rustle in the wind. Chris Beardshaw also points out that the wilderness is an area that is constantly, subtly changing through the seasons. Tony Fry recalls Francis Gibson's love of nature and of the wildness of northern England

An interim stage in the Wilderness, which looked truly wild before weed trees were cleared. This view is from the foot of the yew-arboured viewing platform at the north end of the Dutch Garden.

and the Lake District, and once again laments the loss of those over-grown yew trees.

No one seems quite sure how long ago the names 'Wilderness' and 'Dutch Garden' were first used at Bridge End. Did the idea come to Francis Gibson fully formed, so that he decided one day that he'd like 'a Dutch garden', and another that he must have 'a wilderness'? Wilderness, however, is one of those weasel words of garden history, along with grove, shrubbery, wood and plantation, whose meaning shifts not only from age to age but also from speaker to speaker. What is envisaged in the listener's mind is another matter altogether. Suffice it to say that the original was unlikely to be anything we'd think of as particularly 'wild' today. From the seventeenth century onwards a wilderness seems to have represented anywhere in the garden that shrubs and trees provided some shelter and seclusion, and interrupted a clear view of the surroundings. In Jane Austen's era, a generation before Francis Gibson's, a wilderness was where significant plot developments might be transacted and intimacies exchanged in a degree of privacy. The sedately paced happenings in *Mansfield Park* would not have proceeded far without the wilderness. The seclusion of a wilderness remains essential for all sorts of more recent real-life discussions and liaisons and affairs. Stewart Harding, modern champion of parks for people, recites a string of social benefits. And he cites statistics – such as the romantic fact that 'four out of ten people say that they love one another in a park'. Stewart Harding is witty and impassioned on his soapbox, going on to say: 'Some of us do more than simply declare our love...'

In creating a Dutch garden in the 1830s and 1840s Francis Gibson was being simultaneously old-fashioned and trendsetting. 'Mr Gibson was clearly a man of unusually acute perceptions,' commented *Country Life.* 'At a time when garden design had sunk to a deplorably low ebb, he had the good judgement to

Work in progress on replanting the Dutch Garden, early summer 2003.

fall upon the old traditions.' The old traditions here allude to the formal sixteenth- and seventeenth-century gardens that had been swept away by the landscape movement, variously labelled as French, Italian or Dutch, but came creeping back as nineteenth-century gardeners indulged in revivalist nostalgia. The fashion for Dutch gardens peaked in the 1890s, towards the end of the Victorian age, but the concept was one that Francis Gibson might well have encountered in his reading at the start of the reign. By 1843 a clear definition was being offered by *The Gardener and Practical Florist*:

> Dutch gardens are a combination of small beds of various shapes,
> so arranged as to form in the whole some fanciful or geometric figure,
> of which, each parterre should be planted with only one kind of flower,
> and the flower for this purpose should be very dwarf, so as not to
> destroy the view of the entire figure, which would be entirely spoiled
> by any of the beds containing flowers above 6–8 inches [15–20cm] high.

Dwarf plants such as creeping verbena, pansies and nemophila were suggested as suitable infill. (Later, in December 1860, the *Floral Magazine* added to the list *Ageratum* 'Imperial Dwarf', a new seedling bred by Gibson's conscientious acquaintance William Chater from *A. mexicanum* that helpfully made up for 'the want of a dwarf blue or lavender flower'.)

Perhaps Francis Gibson's inspiration was taken from a real-life example. We know that Gibson visited Levens Hall (near Kendal in what was then Westmorland) in 1834 and thought it 'the most perfect specimen of the kind' that he had ever seen. Presumably it was to the ancient flower parterres and topiary garden dating from the 1690s that he was referring. In 1838 Gibson bought a copy of *Britannia Illustrata,* published in 1728. The Kip and Knyff drawings of early eighteenth-century country houses still surrounded by formal gardens could serve as a pattern book for designs of scrolls and compartments. Books specifically on parterre design were available in the 1830s and 1840s, but the lack of symmetry in the composition of the Dutch Garden at Bridge End is thought to be rather individualistic. 'It was ahead of the general interest

The Dutch Garden at its zenith in the early 1900s. The scene is reminiscent of that at Levens Hall, which Francis Gibson visited in 1834 and which might well have been his inspiration for making this garden.

in topiary beds…and can be seen as a highly imaginative notion of a historical design,' said one modern commentator.

Restoring Detail in the Dutch Garden

No original plans of the Dutch Garden exist. Other sources were examined in an attempt to find a template for restoring the complex layout of topiary, turf, hedges, parterre beds and paths. The first documentary evidence appears some sixty-odd years after the garden was first planted by Francis Gibson, in the form of postcards and photographs taken in the garden in the early 1900s, and others dated 1912. Then, in 1914, a drawing by Gertrude Jekyll was reproduced in the second edition of *Gardens for Small Country Houses* by Jekyll and Laurence Weaver. Jekyll commended the design with her usual sweeping enthusiasm: 'The Bridge End Garden should stimulate any-one who has patience and half an acre [0.2ha] to emulate its charms.'

Jekyll would probably have swept away intrusive trees with equal conviction. With the exponential growth of the unclipped yew trees over half a century or so, much of the ground pattern was blurred by the time restoration began. Little can grow in their dense shade. The painful decision was made to cut back the yews. 'Coppice' is the term they used: a gentle, tentative-sounding word for what turned out to be a drastic felling to leave a mere 3 feet (1m) or so of trunk. In our ignorance we often picture coppiced woodland as airy groves where sweet chestnut or hazel develops bundles of useful rods and poles. When you look up the word it actually means cutting down low in order to promote regrowth. At first the majestic yews were reduced to stumps. Contrary to appearance this was not vandalism, but well-judged arboriculture. Yews are renowned for regenerating when cut hard back, and sure enough within weeks new, green, needle-like leaves were seen sprouting from most of the trunks. The yews received a good feed and the restorers uncrossed a few crossed fingers as the controversial measure showed the first promise of success.

Topiary itself is a controversial topic. People who favour 'natural' gardening regard it as a sort of mutilation. One anthropomorphic view of the unrestored Dutch Garden saw the yew trees as making a bid for freedom. Instead of submitting to the topiary shears, 'the trees had decided to be trees'. The pendulum of fashion in what gardeners do to

Drastically coppiced or stooled, the mature yews that form the main rhythms of the Dutch Garden are beginning to resprout.

trees swings to and fro. Historically topiary included not only the fancy figures mocked by Alexander Pope in the early 1700s, but also a more subtle shaping of specimen trees to 'improve' their form – an idealistic, Neoplatonic attitude to 'nature' involving perfecting the true 'natural' form of a tree or bush by sympathetic topiary. Pope deplored the: 'Ill taste of those who are so fond of Evergreens (particularly Yews, which are the most tonsile) as to destroy the nobler Forest-trees, to make way for such little ornaments as Pyramids of dark-green continually repeated, not unlike a Funeral procession.'

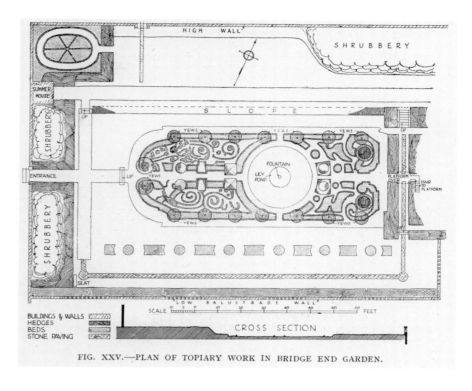

FIG. XXV.—PLAN OF TOPIARY WORK IN BRIDGE END GARDEN.

There is a clear historic precedent for what happened to Bridge End's topiarized yews. Just the same happened to many of the original Jacobean gardens of which the nineteenth-century formal gardens were a revival or re-creation. Those that were not removed outright in favour of a newer fashion became overgrown. In 1721 one John Clerk wrote about 'the evergreen trees and shrubs that were formerly planted in so great numbers that now they grow up and choak the aire'. It is almost with a note of surprise that another writer commented that the yew tree 'arrives at Great Beauty and Value…If not kept down by Formal Clipping.' The trees had decided to be trees. In his excellent *Polite Landscapes* Tom Williamson reminds us of 'the inherent instability' of formal designs, using these examples from the early 1700s, as the first rays of the 'English landscape style' were dawning.

When it comes to restoring the ground pattern of the Dutch Garden using the Gertrude Jekyll drawings, the restoration team find themselves in something of a dilemma. Some of the shapes are a good deal more intricate than their corresponding mirror-images. Chris Beardshaw and Ben Smeeden, the landscape architect who has gardened at Bridge End for twenty years, discuss what to do, which patterns to follow. Was the discrepancy perhaps deliberate, a sense of fun? Unlikely, thinks Chris. His theory is that during the late nineteenth

What Miss Jekyll saw. No original plans for the Dutch Garden survive, and the earliest reference for the restoration team was this drawing made almost three-quarters of a century later by Gertrude Jekyll.

century when the garden was being maintained by a small staff, inattentive pruning led to loss of detail, and that's what Jekyll depicted. The consultants decide to draw up a new planting plan from the part of her drawing that bears most resemblance to the plants that are still *in situ*. Then they flip the drawing over to create the necessary symmetry. Restoration? Reconstruction? The result seems right.

The centrepiece of the Dutch Garden is the pool and its fountain, originally that long-suffering lead Triton that is now kept in a safe place. After due approval by interested parties and the HLF monitor, an appropriate replacement was purchased at Sotheby's. The twentieth-century lead statue of a boy with fish and scalloped shell on a base of three entwined dolphins would almost certainly have been cast from an early nineteenth-century mould, so belongs to Francis Gibson's era. The list of tasks includes relining the pond, installing a pump and putting the statue in place. The pool surround of Portland stone is yet another example of the kind of dilemma that restoration entails. Should they use all new stone, or save one of the eroded original pieces 'for the sake of some intellectual concept of historical continuity'?

When the two types were laid together the visual effect was jarring. New stones were laid; unbroken originals were retained on site, 'so our stance could be reversed at a future time'.

The small celebration arranged to commemorate the switching on of the fountain was a moment of triumph and relief. The water duly emerged and a cheer resounded. Water and wine sparkled. The chairman of the Council, Mike Hibbs, gave a brief speech and everyone raised their glasses and toasted the garden. Here is one community garden restoration where there is no turning back.

In the recent view – besides the replanting – the pool statue has been replaced. The eagle statues decorating the gateposts at the far end are still boxed up for protection.

CHÂTEAU LA CHAIRE
Where Have All the Flowers Gone?

It has the ingredients of a fairy story. Our heroine wanders alone in the grounds of a small château, taking a breather after a long meeting. She considers heading for the seashore invitingly nearby but notices a small wooden gate and the warning that visitors enter 'entirely at their own risk', or words to that effect. She accepts the challenge. Beyond the gate she finds signs of a garden. She explores neglected paths and finds herself amid plants she doesn't recognize, although some of the foliage looks like the sort they use in flower arrangements. (All the best modern heroines take an interest in horticulture: ideally the p's and q's they know include items like *Pinus* and *Quercus*.) She probes further and finds a few other unusual plants, and hints of dramatic landscaping of the precipitous slopes. She finds she has discovered an unknown garden. She has fallen under a spell.

She finds an expert who is able to tell her some of the secrets of the garden's origins, about the man who made the barren valley blossom. There are no flowers here today. What has happened? She wants to know more. She feels the stirrings of a mission coming on.

She finds there are dramatic twists in the plot, like enemy invasion, and she learns of a cameo role played by a visiting exotic princess. But it's still a modern fairy story, and we're still in the early stages. This time the heroine is *outside* the thicket, not imprisoned within it: it is she who intrepidly penetrates the mysterious barriers. She is the rescuer and it is the garden that is to be saved. No fairy godmother has so far appeared. In the process she risks her own fortune: who knows if she and her project will sink or swim?

Hidden? Secret? Lost? A handful of local people have played down the 'discovery' story, protesting that they were perfectly aware of the garden and its famous past all the time. On the other hand, few of them have actually had access to it, and none certainly would have known it in anything like its original nineteenth-century glory. Besides, many of its plants and much of its structure have been hidden or lost. All over the British Isles the middle years of the twentieth century had little sympathy for sprawling old-fashioned high-maintenance gardens

An Outline of the Plot

Until the 1840s La Vallée de Rozel in north-east Jersey was an isolated backwater in a peaceful, rural island we would hardly recognize. Then Samuel Curtis, veteran nurseryman and florist (in the horticultural sense), decided that its microclimate was just what he wanted for growing his collection of tender plants out of doors. Gradually he installed in his chosen spot a house called La Chaire, a widowed daughter called Harriet, an ever-increasing quantity of plants and finally himself. In little over a decade the barren valley was renowned as a plantsman's paradise, and Curtis's experiment in pushing forward the boundaries of horticulture appeared to be a wild success.

So it remained well into the twentieth century, although over time owners and plants variously underwent due processes of change. A flurry of building and replanting activity took place around 1900 at La Chaire. There were periods of enthusiastic gardening. Occupation during World War II marked the demise of the garden's dimming glory, as trees were felled for firewood and plants exported as booty. Minor attempts were made in the later twentieth century to reinstate some of the garden's former brilliance, but it is in the private gardens of neighbours that it's possible to see Curtis's adventurous tradition of plantsmanship living on.

The house that Curtis built was enlarged by subsequent owners to 'château' dimensions. Its use has see-sawed between hotel and private residence in recent decades. Château La Chaire is currently being run as a country-house hotel as a new team of passionate planters enters the garden arena with a restoration mission in mind. The project to breathe new life into the wonderful skeleton of Curtis's garden is in its earliest days. Watch this space.

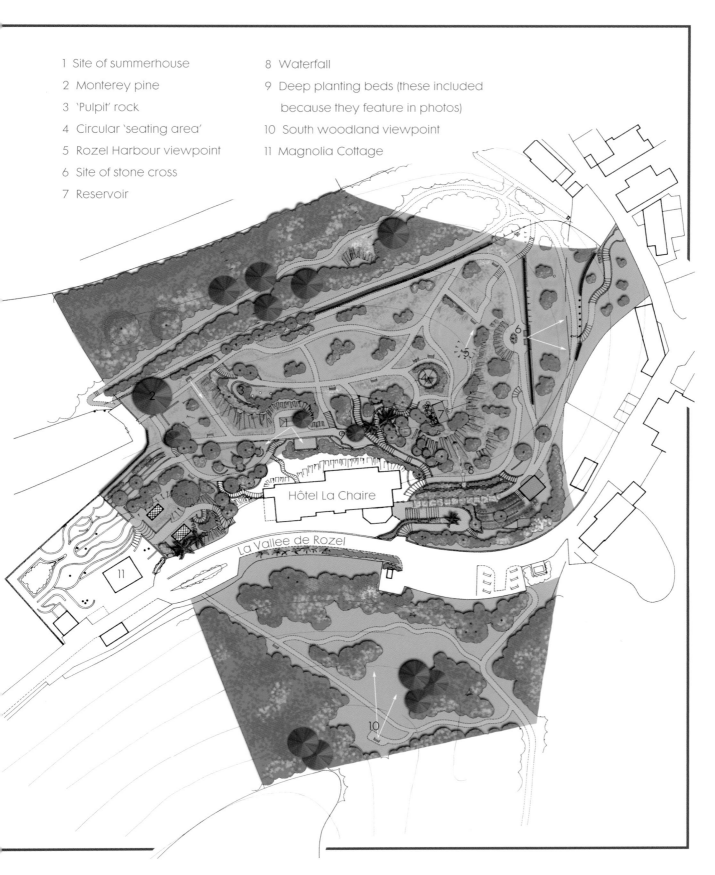

1 Site of summerhouse

2 Monterey pine

3 'Pulpit' rock

4 Circular 'seating area'

5 Rozel Harbour viewpoint

6 Site of stone cross

7 Reservoir

8 Waterfall

9 Deep planting beds (these included because they feature in photos)

10 South woodland viewpoint

11 Magnolia Cottage

Hôtel La Chaire

La Vallee de Rozel

Angie Petkovic' is doing everything in her power to bring about the restoration of the gardens at La Chaire.

that had become overgrown. During World War II this one suffered serious injury. There is much to restore, to repair, to reinstate.

Our explorer is Angie Petkovic', head of a marketing and PR company based in Cheltenham. She was being consulted by the hotel group that owns Château La Chaire when she opened that Pandora's gate. The expert she calls in is Tony Russell, respected in horticultural circles as an authority on shrubs and trees, and more widely known as a gardening writer and broadcaster. As he tells her what he knows about the fame of the man who began this garden, he too falls under the spell. They begin to trace the intervening years of the story and to hatch a plot to rescue the garden.

The Curtis Connections

The Curtises constitute a minor botanical and medical dynasty. The family home was at Alton in Hampshire. Like a number of people we have encountered in earlier chapters, they were Quakers, with parallel pursuits as botanists/apothecaries that blossomed into various careers in horticulture and medicine. In horticultural circles the name Curtis is synonymous with the ground-breaking botanical magazine that is still published today.

Our Curtis was Samuel, the seventh of the eight children of surgeon and apothecary James Curtis, who succeeded his own father John Curtis in the profession at Alton. Samuel was born on 29 August 1779 at Walworth in Surrey, now part of the London borough of Southwark. He seems to have ridden and risen in the wake of his older and better-known first cousin William Curtis (1746–99), who trained as an apothecary and a botanist but made his name with *Flora Londinensis,* published from 1777, and his professional success with the *Botanical Magazine* from 1787. It was later said that the flora gained William Curtis praise, but the magazine brought him pudding. His publications earned him a lasting reputation in serious botanical circles. Inevitably, comparisons have been made between the two 'botanical' Curtises, with Samuel emerging as the lesser man. This is perhaps unfair, since it is not comparing like with like: although Samuel's botanical publications may lack the scientific rigour of William's, his practical achievement as plantsman, florist and nurseryman place him in the first rank of horticulture in the nineteenth century.

My dear Georgiana,
yours affectionately
La Chaire, Rozel,
Jersey, 29 Aug.ᵗ
1858.
Samˡ Curtis.

By 1858, when a series
of portraits was taken at
La Chaire, Samuel Curtis
was 79 and a grand old
man of horticulture. He
dedicated this print to his
daughter Georgiana.

In his publishing bent Samuel seemed to be following in some of
William's footsteps, but in other respects their interests diverged. The
start of the story, however, veers almost towards the incestuous, with
Samuel apparently taking into his hands both William's intellectual
legacy and his only child. William was 'affectionate father to an only
daughter on whom he bestowed a most liberal education'. Samuel
married the orphaned 19-year-old Sarah in 1801. Samuel noted in a

memoir dated about 1859: 'I believe it was a singular fact that my uncle was about 20 years older than my father though but 3 in family. His eldest son William the Botanist was born Jan 11th 1747 at Alton & died in 1799 leaving only one child my late beloved wife.' The union resulted in a bumper crop of progeny, apparently biennials, producing eight girls and five boys of extraordinary longevity, before Sarah died in 1827, having 'contracted a chill in the big conservatory'.

Also in 1801 Samuel Curtis bought a nursery at Walworth. Family connections had provided a useful springboard for his talent. Besides the botanical heritage of his cousin/father-in-law, Samuel learned much from his brother-in-law James Maddock, a neighbouring nurseryman ('florist', Samuel called him) and Quaker who had married Samuel's eldest sister, Mary. After being educated at Ackworth in Yorkshire (like most of his sisters and his brother James), Samuel was apprenticed to Maddock at his Walworth nursery. Samuel developed the Walworth nursery and cultivated a publishing career. First he published some lectures that William had given before his death in 1799. In 1806 he began to publish *The Beauties of Flora*, in an attempt to rival Robert Thornton's successful *Temple of Flora*. The *Beauties* continued until 1820 and featured many plants from his own collection including anemones, auriculas, carnations, dahlias, hyacinths, ranunculus and tulips. These names place Curtis in the mainstream of the florists' tradition. The book is now very rare.

John Brewster discusses one of the plates from Curtis's *Monograph on the Genus Camellia* with Chris Beardshaw. John Brewster's thriving garden at Magnolia Cottage, next door to La Chaire, gives an impression of how the valley was made to flourish in the hands of an expert like Curtis.

Several of its plates were engraved after paintings by Clara Maria Pope, who also illustrated Curtis's *Monograph on the Genus Camellia* (1819). This acclaimed work documented the results of early hybridizing of *Camellia japonica* varieties in the 1790s. Curtis's attachment to the camellia continued throughout his life: he planted them at La Chaire. His attachment to Mrs Pope is not so well documented and, it is suggested, may not have been confined to professional matters.

The daughter of amateur artist Jared Leigh, a youthful Clara Maria married Francis Wheatley some time after 1784. In 1792

Wheatley created the popular *Cries of London* featuring dainty milkmaids, flower-sellers and so on, sold as stipple engravings. His wife modelled for 'his prettier fancy figures'. After his death in 1801 she became the third wife of one Alexander Pope (not the usual Alexander Pope, the poet and aesthete with the garden in Twickenham we encounter in gardening books, but the well-known actor of the day) – perhaps thus honing the 'sense of the dramatic' she displayed in her work. She was more than just a pretty face. She exhibited regularly at the Royal Academy for over forty years. Her earliest work consisted of miniatures, and she was known for her portraits. For a while she painted subjects in a rustic genre with titles such as *Little Red Riding-hood* and *Goody Two-shoes*. However, her vigorous flower portraits earned her admiration and the working relationship with Samuel Curtis has given her enduring fame. The Curtises' daughter born in October 1821 was named Clara Maria in honour of Mrs Pope.

Four of Curtis's other daughters also did botanical paintings in watercolour. Obtaining paintings of the choice blooms from his gardens to be transformed into engravings for his publications was part of Curtis's routine. In the context an invitation to 'come up and see my etchings' by either party would be entirely in order – or we might construe it as the *double entendre* it later became. Will we ever know? Clara Maria Pope died in 1838, and we have to leave the matter dangling as incidental to the La Chaire story, but it might make good material for a novelist or biographer.

In the year 1808 the Society of Arts awarded Samuel Curtis their Silver Medal for 'his exertions in having planted the most extensive orchard in the Kingdom and, also, for his communications to the Society on horticultural matters'. Samuel's expanding botanical collection needed more space and in 1805 he had begun to plant thousands of fruit trees at Glazenwood, near Braintree in Essex. This must have brought him into the same horticultural circles as the Gibson family of Saffron Walden who, like Samuel Curtis, were also Quakers.

While the Glazenwood nursery went from strength to strength, and was succeeded by the La Chaire project, Curtis continued to combine

Lady Guthrie gardens at Les Vaux, further up the valley. Her treatment of a rocky, south-facing slope shows the potential of its microclimate. One of Samuel Curtis's lasting legacies is the tradition of fine plantsman's gardens established in the Rozel valley.

a high-profile practical career with his publishing ventures. His ability as a 'practical arboriculturalist' was highly respected. The Duke of Newcastle employed him at Clumber Park between 1816 and 1821 (where Curtis 'chose for [his] residence Gamston Hall, where Robin Hood was brought up'). In 1845 he was involved in laying out Victoria Park at Bethnal Green, one of London's largest open spaces. He was also appointed to design Nottingham Arboretum in 1850, at the age of 70.

The Move to La Chaire

Jersey beckoned. Curtis explored Rozel in 1841, and bought a parcel of land 'in a bare and rocky valley watered by a stream'. (Actually, according to the records, Thomas Machon sold 'le Mont Crevieu ou Le Chaires' to Harriet Curtis, also known as Mrs Fothergill. Further land was sold in 1844.) Curtis began to build a small square house, at first called Rozel Cottage, near the bottom of the valley and his letters document his involvement in laying out the gardens. He complained of slow progress 'on Act of Labour as we pay a Man 2/– a day for digging', but in fact the house and garden seem to have been set up with remarkable speed.

How much time he spent there during the 1840s is unclear. He was still involved with projects on the mainland, but moved to Jersey permanently in 1852 with his daughter Mrs Fothergill, leaving his son James to take over the Glazenwood business. (No Mr Harriet Fothergill appears in person; the 'eminent' Dr Samuel Fothergill must have died beforehand. Besides keeping house and garden for her father, Harriet busied herself preserving and mounting many of the species of seaweed for which Jersey is noted.)

Had we but world enough and time, it would be intriguing to discover exactly how Curtis came to hear about the Rozel valley. One of the benefits of presenting a TV programme like *Hidden Gardens* as 'work in progress' and sharing the unknowns is that it sometimes prompts readers and viewers to dust off documents in their attics, or inspires a new set of sleuths to follow up minor trails. Somewhere there may exist letters from Curtis himself on the subject, explaining just how it came about. The arguments in its favour must have been persuasive: Curtis wasted little time in securing the property. It seems no coincidence that his friend and colleague Sir William Jackson Hooker himself was in Jersey in 1840 and 1841 with his family. Hooker (1785–1865) was Professor of Botany at Glasgow University before being appointed Director of Kew in 1841, the year Curtis bought La Chaire. He was an accomplished botanical artist and illustrated many of the plates for the *Botanical Magazine*. The Hookers came for the health of their daughter Mary Harriet, who died of consumption and was buried at St Brelade's. However preoccupied he must have been with this family tragedy, Hooker would not have stopped botanizing and garden visiting. The fresh sea air of Rozel Bay would surely lift the spirits of an invalid.

Another likely lead might be Colonel Sir John Le Couteur (1794–1875), 104th and 20th foot, commandant of the Royal Jersey militia and later senior militia aide-de-camp to Queen Victoria. He was elected Fellow of the Royal Society in 1843 and was president of the Royal Jersey Agricultural and Horticultural Society from 1834 to 1839 and it was through his friendship with George IV that the society

Today La Chaire sits against a background of luxuriant vegetation, but this photograph of the original house in 1877 gives an idea of just how steep and rocky the hillside once was.

gained its royal appellation within a year of its founding. Although his literary fame rests on a treatise concerning wheat rather than anything more patently horticultural, he took a keen interest in gardens – both to improve the lot of the lower orders, and also as part of the social life of his peers. In his own fine garden above St Aubin's Harbour he had plants from Kew, where Curtis had been a director, and from the gardens of the Royal Horticultural Society in Chiswick. Curtis and Le Couteur rubbed shoulders at the events of the Royal Jersey Society. Le Couteur also took visitors to see La Chaire, which he variously called 'Italy in Jersey' and more prosaically Curtis's 'pretty rock garden'. 'Harriet and I drove to La Chaire to lunch with Mr Curtis and Mrs Fothergill,' he wrote in 1853, giving a rare glimpse of his human hosts as well as their horticultural environment. 'We were there till 5 looking at his lovely and rare plants, several of which he gave us… He loaded our gig with pretty plants for the wilderness. A fine old patriarch of 83. [Did he mean 73?] Gave my wife his blessings and good wishes for the New Year, and a kiss.'

Warm Jersey for Curtis

The Jersey we know today, so crammed with flowers and tourists that it's difficult to imagine finding a neglected valley into which a new garden might be squeezed with the aid of a shoe-horn, is a comparatively recent phenomenon, a product of later twentieth-century economics. The Jersey Samuel Curtis encountered in the 1840s presented a very different picture. While cider-apple orchards grazed by Jersey cattle covered a quarter of the island, and the potato (not yet the precious 'Jersey Royal') was an established and valuable early-season crop, vast tracts of land lay unexploited. This was the threshhold of the Victorian age with its all-improving ethos and improved (albeit verbose) communications. Horticultural knowledge and ideas were on one level being disseminated by magazines like Curtis's own, and fostered too by bodies like the Royal Jersey Agricultural and Horticultural Society. Five years after its founding, its Annual Report of 1838 was pleased to announce: 'This Society has led to the adornment of cottages; fragrant flowers now decorate many of those yards, which, ten years since, were foul with manure and filth; thus, it has improved domestic economy and cleanliness, and therefore promoted health.'

Much of the hard landscaping visible today on the cliff face above La Chaire dates from around 1900, when the property was owned by Charles Fletcher. Some paths and terracing were created by Curtis, who also increased the growing possibilities by filling crevices and planting pockets with good soil brought up from elsewhere. Fletcher did this on an altogether greater scale. One of the attractions of the unrestored garden today is the way the landscaping articulates the steep slope: steps lure the visitor to ascend and explore, and distant glimpses beckon, inviting discovery.

Agriculture and horticulture, the commercial and the domestic, the useful and the beautiful, went hand in hand in the remit of the Society, and in Samuel Curtis's mind too. Apart from his personal gardening ambitions, Curtis regarded Jersey with all the instincts of the improving Victorian. 'There are many parts in a neglected state capable of growing far more useful things than Furze, Broom and Heath,' he declared, suggesting that the attention of the Royal Jersey Society would be well directed to the improvement of these wastes.' Wishing only 'to be beneficial to its prosperity in Horticulture', Curtis wrote to the Society in 1853 that he thought many parts of the island 'capable of growing the products of the South of France'. Aware that 'the country people are not easily induced to adopt prospective speculations', he was keen for the Society to offer rewards as encouragement in the face of such conservatism. The repeated use of the word 'capable' in the phrases he used to express his desire to tap the potential of the land echoes Lancelot Brown's nickname: a century after 'Capability' Brown, Jersey might have celebrated 'Capability' Curtis.

He certainly impressed islanders and visitors with what he achieved at La Chaire. On 1 June 1855 members of the Royal Jersey Society committee visited La Chaire and reported their surprise 'to see how, in a few years, an unproductive and comparatively barren rock had, under the skilful taste and perseverance of that eminent horticulturist, Samuel Curtis, Esq., become a lovely garden, adorned with beautiful specimens of rare and valuable plants, and is now one of the many attractions of the Island.' La Chaire was a collector's pleasure garden, but some of Curtis's planting embodies a hint of economic botany, an investigation of the 'capabilities' of the climate for useful crops. As well as his ornamental planting, in October 1854 he reported experimenting with sugar ('my sugar cane, sown in April, is eight feet [2.4m] tall, so dense a mass that a cat could not get amongst it') and yams or Chinese potatoes ('I have about 120 pots planted and to plant out, so next winter I hope, if I live so long, to prove their worth'). Plantsmen can never resist a challenge. At the Society's annual dinner in 1886 the lieutenant governor of Jersey produced some samples of tobacco he had himself proudly grown and cured on the island.

'La Chaire' derives from the French term for an ecclesiastical throne or pulpit, or a professorial chair – not to be confused with *chair* meaning flesh (as in *la chair de poule* or goosepimples). The source of

the name lies in the rocky outcrop behind the house that Curtis built, which became known locally as the 'pulpit rock'. Curtis is said to have stood here to preach the word to his gardeners – not a particularly quiet and Quakerly tradition – but by then, perhaps, he had left a lot of that behind. Or maybe he simply stood up and quietly affirmed, just as he might have done when inspired at a Friends' Meeting. On a good day the salient is so near to heaven that it offers any human being a great deal to be inspired about. On a bad day the toughest philosopher will be hard-pressed to note down anything other than the need for more shelter planting.

In the British Isles gardeners are accustomed to finding the most beneficial microclimates along west-facing coasts washed by the Gulf Stream – Cornwall, south-west Eire, western Scotland. A valley running eastwards at the top right-hand corner of Jersey comes as a surprise until we remember we are 100 miles (160km) or so further south than the English coast, at latitude 49 degrees – roughly the same as Paris –

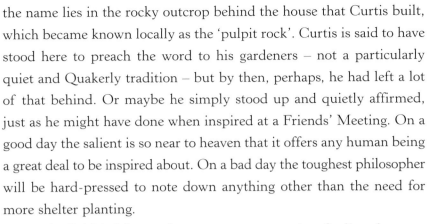

and that Jersey is tucked into the Gulf of St Malo. The valley running horizontally on the map has a steep, rocky, south-facing gradient that catches full sun and a milder, shallower, north-facing slope suitable for woodland under-storey plants. It was often described as a suntrap – the perfect growing conditions for subtropical plants. An over-optimistic assessment, perhaps.

They say Jersey is 'not quite British'. What is decidedly British about the inhabitants is their need to talk about the weather. To experience 'four seasons in a single day' is not an unusual occurrence in an island climate. In the longer term, the unpredictability extends to sudden and pernicious cold snaps and bitter easterly winds. A valley like Rozel is, they say, practically frost-free. Not free, however, from occasional devastating episodes of cold. Curtis experienced these early on beginning with a baptism of fire in 1841. The letter to his son James is written from 'Jersey 11 Feby 1841' (presumably before he acquired Rozel):

> I had supposed from all I heard that a Jersey Winter was a
> very harmless one, & so mild as to let us enjoy out-of-
> doors with but little interruption, however, it is I daresay
> worse than any person on the Island ever before

It's a paradox that the most successful plant colonist at La Chaire today is *Quercus ilex*. The evergreen oak was planted by Curtis towards the exposed top of the site to increase shelter from sea winds. The tree self-seeds freely in the Jersey climate, and in places has regenerated from cut stumps. A priority in restoration is to clear growth from selected areas to reopen key vistas.

remembers it. Last Friday, Saturday & Sunday, we had a frosty easterly wind, attended with a scotch mist & drizzling rain. As fast as it fell it froze on to every thing it touched & the accumulation of the 3 days coated every twig with Ice as transparent as Glass, so that the slender twigs of a Tamarisk opposite to our window were encrusted with Ice an Inch & half [4cm] in diameter, & all the Trees were so loaded in the same manner that the weight of Ice began to break and split the boughs down, & had a brisk wind sprung up every tree must have been ruined. On Monday morning it began to thaw, it was still foggy, & we walked out to see the mischief which was done & still going on, there was previously about 4 Inches [10cm] of Snow on the ground, which was coated with Ice so as to be as sonorous as a drum; in our walk we could hear branches fall ¼ of a mile [0.4km] from us, & so perpetual was the crashes in all directions about us, that it was like listening to the distant discharge of musketry…

Samuel sincerely hoped James had 'not been visited by anything similar' at Glazenwood with its vulnerable orchards and glasshouses.

A year later he was writing to James from 'Rozel Cottage', with the last of the out-of-doors chrysanthemums still on the table. 'Winter has at last set in here with sharp frosts, sleet & slippery roads,' he wrote on 14 January 1842, 'so that it staggers my faith in Australian plants in our fine climate, but still our Valley is beautifully sheltered, the Snowdrops & Primroses &c in bloom.' Curtis calculated that with the aid of perhaps £200 – spent on glasshouses, or some other form of protection? – 'the seasons might almost be defied' in the valley.

Jersey 11. Feb.y 1841

My dear James

I had supposed from all I hear that a Jersey Winter was a very harmless one, so mild as to let us enjoy out-of-doors with but little interruption, however it is I dare say worse on the Island was before remembered Sunday, we had a frosty ca misted drizzling th

In December 1853 Jersey was still 'Paradise' for Curtis. 'We have still many gay flowers & keep up a good show of flowers in our Parlour & we still have near 50 Bunches of good Grapes left in the Greenhouse… our strawberries will keep flowering altho it is very foolish of them, but one has succeeded & brought a fine fruit for Christmas day.'

He was disappointed by the severe winter of 1855. His successor at La Chaire, Charles Fletcher, recorded similar events. A great blizzard destroyed the eucalyptus (described in 1893 as standing 80ft [24m] high above the house – a champion tree?) and other subtropical plants in 1895. Planting around the 'old eucalyptus stump' featured in Charles Fletcher's diary in May 1899, but in December that year he recorded that 'the Gardeners blasted and dug out part of the old Eucalyptus stump'. Gardeners are opportunists: when a tree disappears, it is a chance to use the space for something else.

North-east Jersey is also distinguished by a change in soil type. Whereas most of the island consists of granite, the soil here is a soft purple conglomerate called pudding stone. La Chaire's native pudding stone looks like a coarse concrete with a particularly classy aggregate. Ovoid fruit-like fragments, purple-red igneous rocks ground smooth by aeons, the size of almonds and damsons, dates and plums – and the occasional mango – are embedded in a hard, hard matrix. (When will someone do a Jersey Rock Garden for Chelsea?) Farther south everything is built of pretty, pinkish granite, hewn into rectangular slabs. Occasionally blocks of this intermingle in structures with the pudding stone in the La Chaire gardens. The story of the garden is as studded with succulent horticultural and biographical plums as the pudding stone substrate of the valley itself.

'We have been told that nature had done much for La Chaire. This may be so, but what nature did for the place was by accident. Art, Science and Industry have done the rest, and made a pretty good job of it.'

The Jersey Gardener,
May 1884

Curtis's Garden at La Chaire

Adam White saw Curtis at La Chaire in 1858 and wrote up an account of his visit for the Linnean Society. Curtis had been attracted by the apparently sheltered situation of the bay and thought of it as a place to which he would like to retire. 'For a trifling sum he purchased the rock and immediately began to transform it into a Chinese garden' – was that a quote from Curtis, we wonder, or White's own interpretation? Only 'a scanty sprinkling of rock flowers' grew on the steep bare rock. Curtis quarried out a place to build a house 'and by dint of labour he carried winding walks to the top, and succeeded in bringing up some of the rich vegetable soil of the island, with which he filled artificial fissures and hollows in the rock.' Within a few years La Chaire was covered with a mass of the most varied vegetation. Curtis maintained that shrubs and plants that required the protection of a greenhouse even in the Isle of Wight stood all seasons at Rozel Bay without any injury.

Whereas the geology of most of the island of Jersey is granite, the area around Rozel consists of a coarse conglomerate rock called pudding stone.

This was not entirely true. Some commentators have said Curtis was misguided: Rozel has by no means as favourable a microclimate as one might think. After all, one side of the valley faces north. However, this is precisely the aspect that would suit Himalayan plants such as Curtis's favourite rhododendrons and camellias. Less dramatically cliff-like in its contours, its moister humusy soil seems to be just what ericaceous shrubs would enjoy.

What exactly did Curtis grow? The restoration bid would love to know. No one, apparently, made an inventory during his lifetime. He obtained many plants from his son James at Glazenwood, but few are specified in surviving correspondence. There exist some lists of plants Curtis obtained, or, rather, ordered, from Kew. The best sources may be Curtis's surviving letters, where a thorough toothcombing produces occasional allusions. Early on he thought tree peonies would do well in the deep crevices between the rocks. 'I have more than thirty tall stems of Yucca gloriosa in blossom at once!' he triumphed in 1854. An undated letter mentions dahlias 'on the Top of the Rock' – a planting it is hard to imagine today.

Another source of information about Curtis's plants comes from nineteenth-century descriptions by visitors and commentators. Curtis died at La Chaire in 1860. He was buried in St Martin's churchyard and commemorated in a number of obituaries. His plants, of course, lived on. The short-lived *Jersey Gardener* magazine described the planting at some length in 1884, a generation after his death, when his daughter Harriet Fothergill and her gardener Beckford were in charge (and Curtis's plants were maturing nicely). The rhododendron species were particularly impressive:

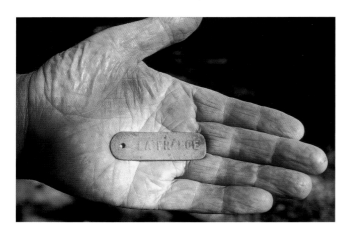

> *Arboreum* 20 feet [6m] high, with its long leaves, dark green above and silver grey beneath, *Falkoneri* from Sikkim, with its hairy leaves and grand yellow flower, growing in the open, and looking as healthy as if on its own native Indian mountains, so is also its neighbour, *Edgeworthii*, and that glorious mass of pink and white, *Formosum*, the great bushes of *Campanulatum*, from Nepaul, are not yet in bloom, nor the equally fine Bootan variety *Jenkinsi*, but a fine hybrid between *Formosum* and *Edgeworthii*, raised on the place is, and as beautiful thing as can be desired.

Finds by amateur metal detectors in the gardens of La Chaire include coins, several bullets and a number of metal labels recording plants that have long since disappeared. This is stamped 'La France', the name of a rose that dates from 1867, but the label is probably far more recent.

There were rhododendrons, but the writer went on to intersperse his commas in a list of some of the other genera making up a horticultural League of Nations – 'all sorts of odds and ends, from all parts of the world…growing on that little patch of semi-barren rock':

> The Acacias, from New Holland, are in great force, large trees and bushes in great variety, and with many other plants from the same part of the world. The Loquat, Eriobotrya Japonica, the China Tea, Thea veridis…the Olea Fragrans…Olea sativa…a New Holland Pepper Tree, Tasmania aromatica, Spiraea grandiflora…Bamboos… Gum trees from Australia, a host of sorts of Mesembryanthemums… bulbous plants from South Africa. Azalias from India and America …

The 'great masses of luxuriant vegetation' – the various shades of grey and green foliage – allowed this commentator only 'an occasional peep of brown rock'. Curtis would have been pleased. In the early years of building and quarrying, as he accumulated 'all the best plants for it', he complained that 'until it is planted it looks like Sebastopol!' The comment was echoed by a new owner in 1901: 'The walls will take a long time to cover…at present it looks more like the ruins of a Roman amphitheatre.' Charles Fletcher's approach was New Money, New Broom. He embarked on extensive rebuilding of house and garden,

An Island Flower

One of the most colourful and unexpected episodes of La Chaire's Victorian heyday concerns a rather unusual instance of the Jersey Royal: in this case not the famous potato selected in 1878 by Hugh de la Haye but a forgotten princess from Hawaii, the island group discovered by Captain Cook in 1778 and named the Sandwich Islands. For a while in the 1890s it was the politics rather than the plants of the Pacific that touched La Chaire.

The last Crown Princess of Hawaii – HRH the Princess Victoria Ka'iulani (1875–99) – came to England for her education and her health. She was an exotic hybrid, half Scottish and half Kanaka Maoli. Her father, the Hon. Archibald (Archie) Scott Cleghorn, married her mother Princess Miriam Likelike (pro-nounced 'leakyleaky') in 1870. Their daughter visited La Chaire several times between 1892 and 1897 in the company of Mrs Fothergill's niece and heir, Mrs Phebe Rooke. The princess actually leased the house in 1896. Her correspondence, unfortunately, contributes little to the horticultural record. 'Mrs Rooke's house is not very large, but her garden is very beautiful,' she wrote home to her aunt, Queen Lili'nokalani. 'The highest point in it is 200 feet [60m], the view from the top is simply beautiful,' she added breathlessly; 'I enjoy walking to the top very much, though it is a very stiff pull up there.' The weather was 'quite perfect' and she thought that the place reminded her very much of home.

The Princess Victoria Ka'iulani in 1890.

She left Jersey in 1897 to campaign for her country's rights in the United States. The campaign failed in the face of gunboat diplomacy and domination by American residents in Hawaii and President William McKinley's political volte-face in his Manifest Destiny. She died in Hawaii shortly after it was annexed by the US in 1899.

It was during her childhood that she met the writer Robert Louis Stevenson, who called her his 'Island Flower'. Later appellations include 'Princess of the Peacocks', 'Hope of a Nation' and 'Heart of the People'. In Hawaii Victoria Ka'iulani is celebrated as tragic cult figure who inspires fact and fantasy and is commemorated in diverse ways from theatrical plots to postage stamps.

and it is his hand that is most evident in the garden structure that remains today (but even his plants have all disappeared).

The Enthusiastic Mr Fletcher

Plants come and go but rocks endure, more or less. Much of the hard landscaping at La Chaire dates from the early years of Charles Fletcher's ownership. He bought the property from Mrs Fothergill's niece and heir, Phebe Rooke, in 1898. Dividing his time between Jersey and Monte Carlo, he has been described as having 'a Mr Toad-like passion' for yachting and the first motorcars. He rebuilt and extended the house that Curtis built. He also tackled the garden, which after fifty years must have needed some refurbishment.

If he had money to splash about, he also had taste – to a degree. He bought choice plants from the best nurserymen of the day in the south of England and in France. Overall he was less adventurous than Curtis, although he did continue the tradition of planting 'exotics' like acacias, palms and bamboos. He mainstreamed on climbers like roses, wisteria, ceanothus, clematis, jasmine and so on. Indeed, to modern gardeners indoctrinated in the Lutyens/Jekyll school of hard structures

Immediately behind La Chaire (but way above roof height) is one of the areas where Charles Fletcher got his builders and gardeners to mould the landscape and improve the planting opportunities. The large raised bed to the right in this view represents a huge feat of engineering.

softened by romantic planting, Fletcher's garden sounds rather good.

Today we'd give him full marks for design in the 'garden structure' department. The way he (or, rather, his intrepid builders) succeeded in running steps up and around the quarried cliff face, and managed to mould soil-filled beds and bracket curvaceous beds between rocky outcrops, is a masterpiece of vertical terrain management. He described his walling as 'Roman ruins' and then paradoxically seems to have wanted to cover it up. The steps invite the visitor to explore, and the rock-cupped beds articulate the scene even when relatively plantless. Filled with Fletcher's planting, they must have looked glorious indeed.

Fletcher's gardening generosity has a spin-off for today's garden detectives. He kept detailed records. His diaries are every restorer's dream, recording building and planting projects, orders and arrivals. He quickly decided to build on to La Chaire instead of building a new house. (The improvements included a new roof, two new bedrooms, offices, a smoking room in place of the old conservatory, a veranda, and a terrace 'with steps up the front'.) He improved views and transplanted plants, perhaps doing things that would have offended Curtis ('the tall Rhododendrons are being cut down to clear the space for the additions to the house'). Gardeners and builders, known by surnames, were variously engaged and sacked. He widened paths, constructed

Since he was called in to advise on the restoration, garden expert Tony Russell has come to know every inch of the site and examined every existing record, but there are still many puzzles. When he and Chris Beardshaw dig down to investigate the large raised bed, they find it brim-full of strange powdery soil, devoid of organic matter.

steps, moved greenhouses, built cottages and stables and planned walls, some with trellis, iron arches or rustic rails. In January 1900 his men were 'hard at work filling up the terraces with soil…we have rigged up a truck on wheels which works on rails and is drawn by a winch'. In April he noted, 'Owing to the Crane working the wall is getting up well'. Technology was also enlisted in the creation of waterworks. The tank built on the hilltop was filled by means of an engine (presumably steam-driven), enabling Fletcher to report that he 'ran waterfall after lunch' on 6 April 1899.

We all know people like Fletcher, who seem always to be tweaking their gardens along with their newly acquired houses. In Fletcher's case we can be grateful that the flow of enthusiasm and expenditure is matched by the flow of information he recorded in the diaries. Armed with on-site dating of certain structures, a determined garden detective could probably join the dots and re-create his entire garden, both hard landscaping and planting.

Today still water gathers duckweed in the pool to the east of the house. Here Charles Fletcher's fountain cascaded or trickled down the cliff from the reservoir above. 'Started the waterfall very slightly on,' he wrote in April 1899, 'and I intend to keep the water just dribbling this way all summer.'

GREGORY & SONS'
"ROYAL BLUE" FOUR-HORSE EXCURSION CARS
START FROM THE
ROYAL LIVERY STABLES, LA MOTTE STREET,
And 14, DAVID PLACE, AT 10.45., RETURNING ABOUT 5.

BY APPOINTMENT   TO HER MAJESTY.

ROUND THE ISLAND DAILY.   FARE, 2s. 6d.   TAKING THE FOLLOWING ROUTES.

MONDAY.	TUESDAY.	WEDNESDAY.	THURSDAY.	FRIDAY.	SATURDAY.
Gallows' Hill, (West Mount)	Manning's Residence,	* Special Trip.	Queen's Road,	Government House,	La Haule Manor,
Mont Cochon,	Beaumont Village,	Beaumont,	Zion Cemetery,	St. Saviour's Church, 1154.	St. Peter's Church, 1167,
St. John's Lane,	La Haule,	St. Aubin's Bay,	Proscrit's Obelisk,	PRINCE'S TOWER.	Augerez,
Houge Boëte Manor House,	North-West Arsenal,	" Town and Fort,	BONNE-NUIT BAY,	Peacock Trees,	Vinchelez Manor,
CREUX DU VIS, OR DE-VIL'S HOLE,	St. Peter's Church, 1167,	ST. BRELADE'S BAY,	Mont Mado Quarries,	BOULEY BAY,	" Lane,
* GRÈVE DE LECQ,	" Vineries,	St. Brelade's Church, 1111,	Stones Procured for Thames' Embankment,	* ROZEL BAY,	* PLÉMONT,
† CAVES,	Augerez,	Fishermen's Chapel, 786,	St. John's Church, 1412,	TROPICAL GARDENS,	† " CAVES
St. Mary's Church, A.D. 1320,	St. Owen's Schools,	Les Creux Fantômes,	* GRÈVE DE LECQ,	Rozel Manor,	View of all Channel Islands,
Six Roads,	Vinchelez Manor, " Lanes,	West Point Battery,	† CAVES,	St. Martin's Church, 1116,	GRÈVE AU LANÇON,
St. Lawrence Church, 1199,	* Plémont,	Corbière Rocks and Light-house,	St. Mary's Church, 1320,	Mount Orgueil Castle,	Grosnez Point,
Mont Félard.	† Caves,	La Rocco Tower,	Six Roads,	Gorey Village,	Ruins of Grosnez Castle,
	St. Owen's Church, 1130,	St. Owen's Bay and Lake,	St. Lawrence Church, 1199,	Grouville Bay,	New Wesleyan Chapel,
	St. Peter's and St. Lawrence's Valleys,	Kempt Tower,	Mont Félard or Cambrai.	Race-course,	A Good Drive Home.
	Vineries.	* L'ETACQ,		Grouville Church, 1322,	
		St. Owen's Manor,		Longueville Manor,	
		Bel Royal, late residence of Charles II.			
		Millbrook.			

THESE ARE THE ONLY EXCURSIONS ALLOWED THE PRIVILEGE OF VISITING ROZEL MANOR GROUNDS.

* Lunch provided.   † When the tide permits.

THE CARS WILL CALL FOR PERSONS STAYING AT PRIVATE APARTMENTS, IF DESIRED.
Campbell, the Guide, will Play on an English Concertina, made expressly for him by the celebrated Louis Lachenal, of London, and also entertain the Excursionists by Singing several of the first Songs of the day.

Abier Bros., Printers, New Street, Jersey.

In his notes on purchasing plants, Fletcher namedrops a number of major nurserymen of the time. Deciding to cover the new walk with clematis, he wrote for Jackmann & Sons' catalogue. In January 1900 he 'Wrote to Cutbush for Laburnum, Rhus cotinus, Mays, Tulip trees. Wrote to Veitch for Japanese Cherries and Flowering Peaches, Vines etc.' Veitch's received frequent orders. At one point Fletcher considered getting the firm to lay out the garden, but changed his mind when he heard: 'They want to send a Landscape Gardener and probably make an expensive job of it.' In October 1900 he 'planted the Delphiniums from Kelway'; next year he was ordering peonies, asters, gaillardias, pyrethrums and *Physalis franchetii* from the firm. From Cant of Colchester he obtained large numbers of roses, but the twenty 'Maréchal Niel' he bought 'for walls alongside the paths in the new Garden' were found to be suffering from canker two years later. Other well-known garden suppliers are mentioned: Pulham and Sons were consulted about making a small waterfall in artificial rock and Boulton and Paul supplied a 'large fowl house' for his wife Ethel's black Orpingtons. It all amounts to a wonderful picture of what was desirable in a country garden at the turn of the century.

Towards the end of the 1800s the 'Tropical Gardens' of Rozel Bay were among the principal tourist attractions of Jersey. This advertisement includes them in its programme for Friday. It came to an end in 1899, when Charles Fletcher 'Wrote to Down's and Gregory's Stables and to the Rozel Hotel saying that the La Chaire Gardens are in future closed to the public.'

The Aftermath: a Dying Fall

After World War I the estate had a chequered history. While the house
flourished, the garden declined. Fletcher sold up in 1921. New owners
from 1932 were the Nicolle family and the garden blossomed again
under the stewardship of Mrs Nicolle. Family photographs of the
garden include a picture of *Magnolia campbellii* in flower near
Magnolia Cottage, reputed to be the finest specimen in Europe. The
tree was presumably planted during Mrs Fothergill's tenure, since it
was introduced from the Himalayas only eight years after Curtis died
in 1860. In 1933 an eminent visitor to La Chaire was Charles Raffill of
Kew, who later produced *Magnolia* 'Charles Raffill' by crossing forms
of *M. campbellii*. The fifteen-year Nicolle ownership was interrupted
by the German Occupation. A professional gardener looked after the
gardens, but there were predators other than the usual pests and diseases. Two tales hang thereby. The first is generally vague: trees were
cut down for firewood. The second has a specific letter as its source.
German officers gave instructions that certain plants should be packed
up to be sent to Germany (where, presumably, they were destined for
the shelter of someone's glasshouse, or a botanical garden). Reporting
on the execution of this order, gardener Mr Le Bloas wrote to Mrs
Nicolle that he had 'given the plants a last watering...of *acid*'.

After 1947 the property went through a chain of owners and some
was sold off. Only occasional references to the gardens appeared in
print: plants were recorded in 1979, and some attempt at new planting
was made towards the end of the 1980s. In recent years only the
immediate surroundings of the hotel have been maintained: the wider
ramifications of the garden have reverted to nature.

The Vision

The project to garden again at La Chaire is in its very early stages: the
picture Chris Beardshaw presents is very much the 'before' version of
the hoped-for transformation. According to the Landsberg criteria
discussed in the first chapter, neither reconstruction nor restoration in
the strict sense is feasible at La Chaire: there is insufficient information
about what Curtis planted, and where. The garden evolved dramatically
in its first fifty years, but the existing layout and elaborate structures

certainly owe more to Charles Fletcher than to Samuel Curtis. Fletcher, too, was an innovator, who laid a personal stamp on the planting. Working in the footsteps of an enterprising and adventurous plantsman poses particular dilemmas. Neither Curtis nor Fletcher would have allowed their garden to stand still: they would always have been experimenting with new plants. Failures would be seen as part of a learning curve and would have prompted a search for alternatives or even a change of direction.

A creative solution by a visionary plantsperson must be the best, though controversial, solution for such a site. Many plants associated with Curtis would, of course, be on the essential plant list. But an innovative strategy in the spirit of Curtis and Fletcher should be allowed. One idea is to respond to the varying microclimates offered by the rocky slopes and to plant the different habitats accordingly with exotics from different parts of the world. The notion of a subtropical 'hanging garden' has been mentioned. Another wonderful island garden, Tresco, in the Scillies, has been held up as a potential touchstone.

For all the philosophizing about the planting approach, reinstating visitable gardens at La Chaire entails a great many practicalities. The fairytale project needs to find solid support in a dozen spheres, not least financial. Samuel Curtis was not exactly single-handed in creating his garden at La Chaire, but his was an age when a wealthy eccentric could pursue an idea, take risks and achieve transformations on a scale unimaginable today. It's a paradox that while we have the machinery to do in an hour what men with shovels and pickaxes took days to do in the 1850s, today's visionaries have to spend unforeseeable lengths of time in planning and consultation, negotiation and diplomacy, business plans and feasibility studies. Samuel Curtis set an inspiring precedent: it will be a fitting tribute if this early landmark on Jersey's garden map can be made to flower again.

One way or another, La Chaire's exotic quality and atmosphere must be resurrected and reanimated. Enthusiasm once won the day – 'La Chaire...may be termed a wonderful proof of what taste and skill can effect.' Can enthusiasm conquer again?

The lower slopes of the north-facing side of the valley are not only shady but also moistened by the tiny stream at the bottom, making another distinct habitat for plants.

GREENWAY
Planted Treasure in a Riverside Plot

It is hard not to name-drop at Greenway. Whether it's Dame Agatha Mary Clarissa Christie (née Miller, later Mrs Max Mallowan 1890–1976), Queen of Crime-writers, or *Paulownia tomentosa* 'Lilacina', Sir Walter Raleigh (1582–1618), courtier, navigator and poet, or John Charles Williams (1861–1939) of Caerhays Castle, who sponsored plant collector George Forrest and acquired Ernest Wilson's plants via Veitch's celebrated nursery, and who bred the eponymous *williamsii* camellias.

Plant pedigrees: in between the name-drops it is hard to avoid the lists. Lists of plantsman's plants are routine here and in Greenway's cousin-gardens such as Caerhays: to the enthusiast, protocols and pedigrees in plant breeding are quite as important as in human families. Every component of the long botanical name specifying precise parentage of each hybrid and variety is noted and relished like some plant peerage or Almanach de Gotha. Plants at places like Greenway are designer babies, bred for specific attributes.

There are lists of owners, too: this is an estate that has changed hands many times. Even the owners' names change, as an absence of direct heirs causes the descent to slip sideways – Roope Harris adds on a second surname to become Roope Harris Roope; Marwood is hyphenated on to Elton. Many owners have other estates, and move to and fro and these off-stage sites are important for garden historians to study in case they show stylistic influence, and later because their gardens make important parallels (Cornish Trewidden and Caerhays in particular). Between the lines were periods when the property was let out, or bought perhaps speculatively and sold on rapidly.

You may come to Greenway with a full panoply of maps and lists and lenses: binoculars to spot the egrets on the far shore; a hand-lens to examine the details of the rare plants; reading glasses to scrutinize the lists of plant names. Pause for a moment. Make yourself forget names and words. Close your eyes and open them again, and open yourself to all the different sensory impressions this beautiful place will awaken. Visit Greenway and enjoy the scents, breezes, light and

An Outline of the Plot

Greenway, on the river Dart, has seen the best part of 500 years of gardening of one sort and another. We know nothing of the gardens that must have surrounded the house built by the Gilberts in the reign of Elizabeth I. It was replaced by the present house in around 1790, and a sweeping new garden layout in the style of Humphry Repton was made at about the same time. Much of this framework can still be traced on the ground, but documentation is tantalizingly rare – perhaps because the estate is a small one, passed through many different hands.

The lack of historic documentation contrasts with a plethora of detailed plant records and descriptions as Greenway became the property of a succession of keen plantspeople including, since 1938, the family of Agatha Christie. Plants not entirely hardy elsewhere can thrive at Greenway in the favourable microclimate of south Devon and the shelter of the Dart estuary. Several owners had connections with Cornwall, and with famous Cornish gardens. The planting

The scandent climber *Tibouchina urvilleana* attempts to escape from one of the glasshouses at Greenway.

legacy of owners connected with Carlyon of Tregrehan, Williams of Caerhays and Bolitho of Trewidden consists largely of collections of exotic shrubs and trees, many from the southern hemisphere, which have gradually transformed the parkland of the Reptonian layout into a woodland setting.

The estate of 270 acres (109 ha) was given to the National Trust in 2000. The Trust aims to keep the garden looking as if it is 'poised on the edge of wildness' while nurturing its plant legacy. One remit is to repair paths and structures and unobtrusively make the garden more accessible to visitors. Two particular areas have been of special interest to Chris Beardshaw and the team. They have helped restore a piece of pure Victoriana in the form of an intimate little garden of rocks and ferns. They have also explored the much longer and more puzzling history of a walled garden whose associations stretch from the Spanish Armada to Agatha Christie herself.

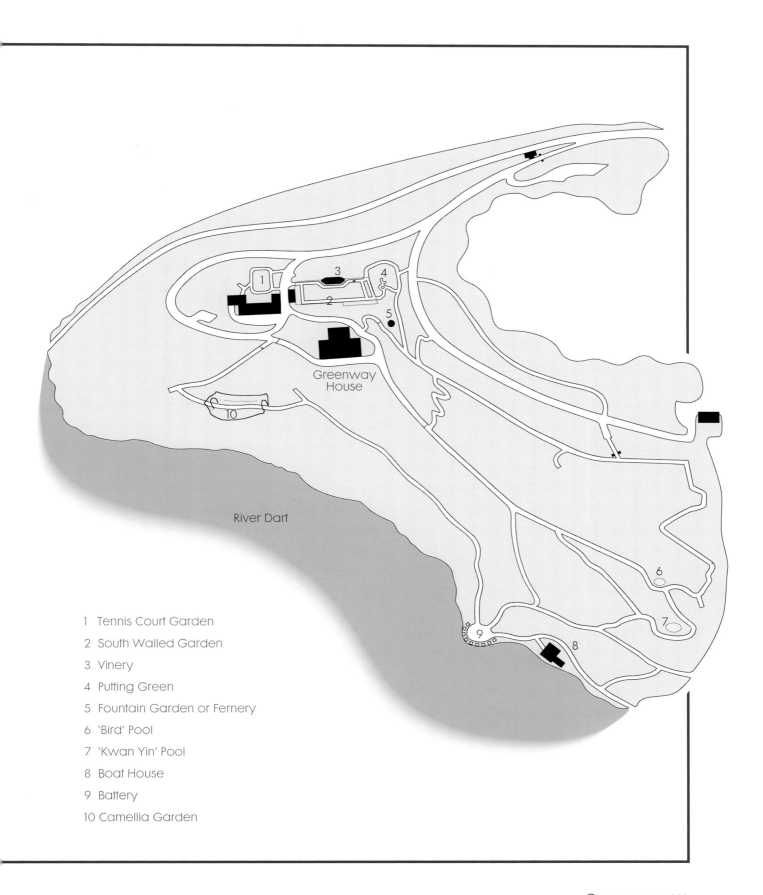

1 Tennis Court Garden

2 South Walled Garden

3 Vinery

4 Putting Green

5 Fountain Garden or Fernery

6 'Bird' Pool

7 'Kwan Yin' Pool

8 Boat House

9 Battery

10 Camellia Garden

Greenway House

River Dart

Greenway's Owners

The Gilberts	1600s
The Roopes (Cabell, Deeble, Harris)	c1700–91
The Eltons (Marwood-Elton)	1791–1832
The Carlyons	1832–51
The Harveys	1851–82
The Bolitho and Williams families	1882–1937
Agatha Christie	1938–59
Mrs Rosalind Hicks, Anthony Hicks and Matthew Prichard	1959–2000
The National Trust	2000 onwards

shade, as well as the sights and the views. Absorb that important 'sense of place'. Marvel at the steepness of the site and the sudden glimpse between the trees of light reflected from the river, like sky in the wrong place.

This, however, is a book, and in between the pictures, words and names are our medium. We'll focus on people and plants: the significant owners, the ones who collected the best plants, and the ones who made most impact on the appearance of the site. Chris Beardshaw's business, too, is plantsmanship, and he relishes the plant-collection aspect of Greenway. 'Three different paulownias!' he says excitedly as he points to a group of foxglove trees planted close enough together for the differences and similarities to be compared. 'Five different michelias!' he exclaims with the enthusiasm some chaps reserve for a classic car. A visit to Greenway should be a compulsory part of the curriculum for all students of horticulture and taxonomy. But even they should take time to marvel at the beauty and atmosphere of the place.

Of Time and the River

The Greenway garden is about landscape, not landscape in the aesthetic eighteenth-century sense as at Croome, but pure down-to-earth topography, where landforms perforce dictate human movements. Or waterforms, rather, since it is water that carved the shape of this estuary. It was by water, of course, that past inhabitants travelled and ferried their goods, far more efficiently than overland. It is inviting to arrive by ferry today – a 'green way' to arrive at Greenway, and an approach that puts the visitor better in touch with the history of the site than squeezing four wheels down narrow, twisting, landlocked lanes.

You can see at a glance the effect of the river on the vegetation and land use. Natural oak woodlands shroud the shores that are too steep to cultivate (unless you have a few Spanish prisoners of war to set to

Seafarers have brought adventure as well as plants to Greenway. The river Dart affects the garden's microclimate in this sheltered corner of south Devon. This is the view upstream towards Dittisham from near the Greenway boathouse.

work), in the same way that seaweed clothes the domed rocks exposed at low tide. The rounded tree crowns are the dabs of a paintbrush. By contrast the Greenway stretch of riverside has woods of a different texture, calling for light brushstrokes of bluer green for feathery cryptomerias, cypress and pines, and blobs of glossy deeper green for the shiny dark leaves of understorey shrubs like camellias and iteas.

Just as the terrain reflects the water's shaping, so the climate is modified by the water's proximity. Greenway has a sheltered west-facing aspect, and the curving estuary protects it from south-westerly salt winds. Like those of Samuel Curtis at La Chaire, a gardener's eyes light up at the planting 'capabilities' of such a site. For the garden designer, or the eighteenth-century 'improver' intent on creating a landscape to impress, the prospects are more challenging. Even Capability Brown would have had his work cut out.

The house was built around 1790. Still in private hands, it can only be glimpsed from the pleasure grounds by visitors.

The river Dart contributes hints of danger and adventure, fictional and actual. Old rhythms come into your head like 'Brandy for the Parson/'Baccy for the Clerk'. Greenway has its gun batteries and cannon (saluting ones), but real cannon guarded the riverside during the Napoleonic wars. Little boats from the Dart and their crews played a part in the Dunkirk rescue. The estuary was an anchorage for landing craft assembling for the invasion of Normandy in 1943.

In historical times, the tides have lapped the story of Greenway from the era of the seafaring Gilberts, and the sea has brought Greenway plants of many kinds. Otho Gilbert built the first house in the late sixteenth century. His sons were Humphrey, who was knighted for establishing the colony of Newfoundland, and John, deputy-lieutenant of Devon, who at Greenway benefited particularly from the defeat of the Spanish Armada in 1588. (A fellow deputy complained of his using some 160 prisoners of war from the Armada ship *Nuestra Senora del Rosario*, 'every day hardly labouring in his garden in the levelling of his grounds' before they were ransomed and sent home. Level areas are at a premium in terrain like this – and terraced gardens would have been fashionable. We'll

'As Sir Walter Raleigh was smoking his pipe at Greenway, a servant threw a bucket of water over him, thinking he was on fire.'

Local legend

hear a little more about what the Spanish sailors did later.) The Gilberts' half-brother Walter Raleigh was famous in many ways, though his 'plant introductions' – tobacco and potatoes – affected Greenway little.

A complicated series of eighteenth-century owners involved the Roope family of Dartmouth, who were engaged in the triangular shipping trade of exported manufactured goods and cloth, Newfoundland fish and Portugal wines. Roope Harris, born in Boston, Massachusetts, probably imported camellias as well as fortified wine from Oporto, tacked on his Roope surname on inheriting in 1771, and built the house around 1780. He was succeeded by a Bristol merchant venturer, Edward Elton, who built a new house and redesigned the landscape in the style of Humphry Repton to include curving drives, ornamental gardens, a 'ladies' garden' and so on. We'll look more closely at the Eltons' landscaping shortly: it is refracted best from information dating from the 1830s onwards.

After this the owners' wealth derives from landbased incomes: they were the tin-mining Carlyons, the copper-smelting Harveys and the banking and smelting Bolithos. The wealth of Greenway also switches to plants. The sea brought plants from distant climates – from China, Australasia, Chile – to gratify several generations of impassioned plantsmen and gardeners.

The Carlyons in Cameo

The tithe apportionment of 1839–42 with its map and schedule showing individual parcels of land is one of the most valuable tools in helping to reconstructing a picture of Greenway in the first half of the nineteenth century. Better still, Edward Carlyon commissioned a coloured version of the tithe map for himself around that time, which shows the garden right down to individual beds. Carlyon's version of the map used the same parcel numbers as the tithe schedule. The accompanying cartouche showing the front of the house and its immediate pleasure grounds is both delightful and informative, confirming the fashionable 'Reptonian' design.

By comparing this evidence with the first extant estate map drawn for Edward Elton in 1791 and with documentation from the sale of the house in 1832, garden historians have deduced that the appearance of the landscape was largely the creation of the Eltons, and that the Carlyons changed little. They just added plants.

Edward Carlyon bought the estate in 1832. The sale particulars of 1832 for an estate 'exceeding 150 acres [60ha]' must once have been linked to a map or plan that has not survived. Apart from a farmyard that 'encloses every building essential to the purposes of husbandry', specific items mentioned included an 'extensive kitchen garden of 1 acre [0.4ha]', a melon ground, flower gardens, boat house, cold swimming bath and 'Gardener's rustic abode'. The sale particulars described the mansion as 'chaste and uniform… placed on a park of much natural beauty; its spreading foliage and the delightful and rare inequality of the grounds, are protected by hills of fearful height on one side while the other extends to the almost impervious woods and plantations which gently recline to the water's edge.'

The Carlyons owned Greenway between 1832 and 1851. There were eight surviving sons. The older children were born before this, in the

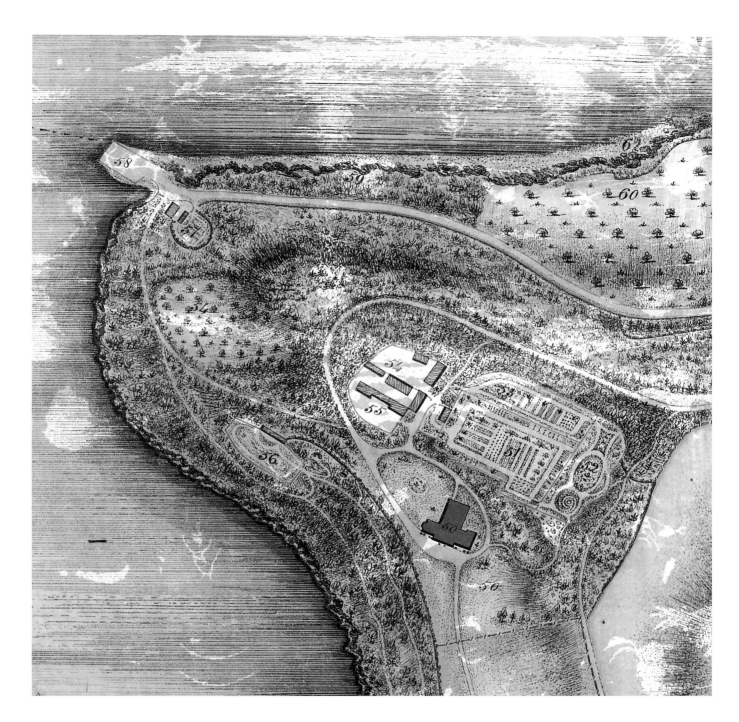

Numbered areas relevant to the history of the garden include:

50 'Greenway House Pleasure ground and shrubbery'

51 & 53 Walled kitchen gardens with beds but no glasshouses

52 Scheduled as 'Garden'; includes the later Fountain Garden or Fernery

54 & 60 Orchards

55 Yards, offices, etc.

56 'Greenhouse & garden', later known as the Camellia Garden

57, 58 & 59 Quay for Dittisham Ferry; Ferry Cottage & Ferry Plantation

Edward Carlyon commissioned a graphic depiction of Greenway based on the tithe map of 1839. Numbers just visible on this section of the map refer to parcels of land listed in the tithe schedule.

GREENWAY HOUSE, SOUTH FRONT.

early 1820s, and among the breathless, unpunctuated 'etcetera' list of the younger 'Richard Samuel Anna William Horatio Arthur Tredenham' in the family tree may be the young persons depicted in the cartouche.

If every family who owned or occupied Greenway proved to be as interesting as the Carlyons, there might be much material for some long-running period soap-opera-cum-country-life saga. The second son (a military man) of a family that had made money from Cornish tin, Colonel Edward Carlyon bought Greenway in 1832 (was he impressed by the effusive sale particulars?). He had married Anna Maria Spry of Place in Roseland, Cornwall. Excerpts from surviving letters make Anna sound more than usually unpredictable. 'I am convinced,' she writes at one point, 'that no place in the world will suit me so well as Greenway.' She plans to 'take a great pleasure in common green house plants' and observes her sons 'collecting chestnuts, fir cone seeds &c to plant at Greenway'. Later letters show a different attitude: 'I am convinced…that Greenway will be a curse on us…I have a perfect horror of the place…I'm sure I never was so unhappy in my life…it is the most gloomy place I ever saw.'

Edward Carlyon had other challenges too. He had to take over running the Tregrehan estate of his older brother as early as 1836, when William was committed as a lunatic. Eventually it was because of his brother's death in 1841 that Edward gradually concentrated on and eventually took over Tregrehan and gave up Greenway. He moved his family to Tregrehan in 1848, along with a number of plants and cuttings.

Mr Harvey Changes the Trains

The estate was briefly owned by a Mr Luttrell, who sold it on almost immediately: an instance of one of Greenway's hidden owners. On Wednesday 2 June 1851 John Culpitt the gardener showed 'every part of the estate and buildings' to Mr and Mrs Richard Harvey and found 'they were hiley pleased with it'. Harvey bought Greenway at auction in 1852. A copper magnate of St Day in Cornwall, Harvey was related to the famous Williams gardening family of Caerhays through his aunt Catherine, who married John Williams and whose son Michael bought Caerhays Castle in 1853.

Records relating to the Harveys' ownership of Greenway show them modernizing and expanding the estate. Oblique references indicate that the garden was evidently thriving. The gardener J. Couldrey recorded some of the fine exotics growing at Greenway in a letter to the *Gardeners' Chronicle* of 3 April 1852. There were several mature acacias, myrtles and a couple of sophoras (then known as *Edwardsia*), as well as *Clianthus puniceus* and *Metrosideros floribunda*. The Ordnance Survey first edition 1:2500 map of 1865 reveals further changes. New glasshouses appear in the walled garden and elsewhere:

Opposite The pictorial cartouche added to the decorative version of the 1839 map confirms the lay-out of the garden to the south of the house and underlines its 'Reptonian' flavour, with miniature parkland noted as 'lawn' in the schedule. The figures depicted in front of the house might represent the younger members of the Carlyon family's eight children.

one is the vinery, still extant but badly needing restoration, while the glassed area was removed from the Camellia Garden – (see page 134).

One important contribution Richard Harvey made to the Greenway estate is precisely a hidden one. In 1861 the Dartmouth & Torbay Railway Company proposed to route the line from Churston towards the Greenway–Dittisham Ferry over Greenway land. Eventually a bridge might be built over the Dart and the line continued through the South Hams to Plymouth. Harvey fought the proposal tooth and nail in the House of Lords and succeeded. The railway was rerouted through a tunnel towards Kingswear. By a nice twist of fate this is one of the few remaining rural lines today, and is run by the Paignton & Dartmouth Steam Railway. Richard Harvey thus retained the peace of Greenway, and the distant toot of the steam whistle evokes a pleasant nostalgia rather than annoyance today.

Richard Harvey left everything to his wife Susannah, including 'my greenhouse and other plants and flowers ' and 'garden tools utensils and implements including the steam engine thrashing machine'.

The gardens around the house at Greenway seem to specialize in doorways and openings that entice you to explore. Here it is the shade and light of the Fountain Garden or Fernery that beckon.

Victorian Values

Just outside the main walled garden is an intimate, inward-looking area, known as either the Fountain Garden or the Fernery. This little secret garden was created – or adapted – by Susannah Harvey after her husband's death in 1870. (She also built the Church of England Primary School at Galmpton and completed the walls of the nursery garden.) It occupies an area shown on Edward Carlyon's map of 1839 as a kind of spiral pattern that could be read as a snail mount. This twilight area between sun-filled functional walled gardens and woodland (or wilderness) must always have been a transitional point in a garden tour. The garden's centrepiece is a circular pool with a tiered cast-iron Coalbrookdale fountain, thought to be pre-1839. Around it a labyrinth of twisting paths radiates between large rocks covered in ivy, saxifrage – and ferns.

The endpiece of Shirley Hibberd's *Fern Garden: how to make, keep, and enjoy it; or, Fern Culture Made Easy* illustrates his ideal of a shady outdoor fernery 'planted with ferns severally adapted to the sites and positions the scheme affords'.

The garden can be seen as gloomy or atmospheric according to the mood and taste of the observer – and perhaps what the sun happens to be doing at that moment. Dogs' graves nearby help the spooky or sentimental resonance, if you like to see it that way. Animal graveyards are a feature of many old gardens, but the dates on these stones are from the 1970s and '80s.

A fern garden is a pure piece of Victoriana, the fresh-air equivalent of the heated indoor fernery – both are relics of a past passion that ecologists of today frown on, like fur coats, or keeping ornamental pheasants in an aviary. (The Harveys did grow tender ferns in the new vinery/conservatory in the walled garden: a fine specimen of *Adiantum farleyense* was noted in *The Garden* in 1901.)

The Victorian fern craze began in the 1830s and early books on ferns pandered to the unfortunate passion. They helped identify species and advised on collecting specimens for pressing and mounting, but also provided tips for cultivation. Rare ferns had been collected by botanists and herbarium collectors for a couple of centuries, but by the nineteenth century they were being plundered on a huge scale to fuel the trade established by itinerant fern vendors, and some of the rarer species came close to extinction in the wild. The sad fact is that they were often sold in cities where – even if they transplanted satisfactorily – they would soon succumb to the polluted atmosphere. This at least

Opposite The Fountain Garden in early summer achieves that desirable designer look common to prefaded denim and distressed new paintwork; it looks so natural as to be *almost* wild.

Replanted Ferns

Greenway's fern garden had become overgrown and very few ferns survived except the coarser common species. Nick Haworth's shopping list included the following:

Asplenium scolopendrium
Athyrium filix-femina 'Frizelliae'
Athyrium niponicum 'Pictum'
Cyrtomium falcatum
  'Rochfordianum'
Cyrtomium fortunei
Dryopteris affinis 'Askew'
Dryopteris erythrosora
Dryopteris goldieana
Matteuccia struthiopteris
Polystichum munitum
Polystichum polyblepharum
Polystichum setiferum
Polystichum setiferum
  Acutilobum group

Japanese painted fern,
Athyrium niponicum 'Pictum'.

would not be a problem at Greenway, where the quantities of lichens encrusting the trees is a sign of the pure air.

Shirley Hibberd, whose bestselling books pandered to many aspects of the growing Victorian market in consumer gardening, claimed to 'believe no one can thoroughly enjoy or understand ferns until after having actually hunted for them…' In *The Fern Garden: How to Make, Keep and Enjoy it; or, Fern Culture Made Easy* he provided clear instructions on the best tools for gathering them, the best way of transporting them home, and how to care for them. 'If you cannot go collecting you may be able to dip into the tempting basket of the itinerant fern vendor,' he added. If he veers on the politically incorrect on the plant-collecting side, Hibberd's surprisingly up to the minute in suggesting 'cocoa-nut fibre' as an alternative planting medium to leafmould or peat.

Outdoor ferneries should 'provide as many aspects and degrees of declivity as possible within certain limits'. The Greenway version with its different mini-microclimates must have fulfilled this excellently. (Hibberd ebulliently expressed his notion of an ideal environment as 'throw[ing] myself into a gravel pit', where he would presumably erect the requisite rocky structures in the shady and damp but well-drained conditions where ferns from a variety of natural habitats might thrive.) Aware that many readers were shrouding their piano legs in skirts and creating dizzyingly coloured patterns with their Berlin woolwork and their summer bedding, Hibberd issued a useful piece of advice. 'Aim at wildness and apparent neglect in the arrangement up to a certain point. Dirt and disorder are as injurious to the ferns as to the morals of those who encourage such things, but primness is not desirable in a fernery.'

Fortunately fern nurseries now propagate plants by modern methods, and the National Trust's 'peat-free' policy means that the restoration of the Greenway garden is beyond ecological reproach.

The Camellia Garden

About halfway downhill between the house and the river lies a unique, discrete garden area. It's the sort of small, enclosed ornamental plot some distance from the house that might have been created as a 'ladies' garden' around 1800, in Humphry Repton style. It is not particularly

Above The puzzling smaller niche with tap and basin is thought to belong to a former aviary on the site.

Left The Camellia Garden has long been a landmark in the garden, and put Greenway firmly on the garden history map with its place in the story of camellia growing in Britain. The rear wall once supported a glasshouse for supposedly tender camellias and later an ornamental niche was created.

prepossessing in appearance, but makes an important contribution to Greenway's story. Maybe it should be glorified with the garden-history term 'palimpsest', as discussed on page 22; or perhaps unravelling its significance will increase its resonance to the unimpressed visitor. It is the sort of thing any garden restoration team needs to investigate to explain the way the evidence has been pieced together.

It is currently labelled the Camellia Garden, and the National Trust's helpful notices describing work in progress put it into some kind of focus for the visitor. 'The Camellia Garden,' A garden detective might query 'But how long has it gone under this name?' It seems variously to have been known as the Battery Garden and the Greenhouse Garden – both names that also apply to other garden areas. 'Can we be sure we're investigating the same plot?' The 1832 sale particulars mention a conservatory. The tithe map of 1839 and Carlyon's commissioned plan show a 'barrel-shaped garden' and the schedule describes the space as 'Greenhouse and garden'. It also contained a pheasantry or aviary: rather a small one, to all appearances. Writing to Edward Carlyon in 1851, Stone the gardener mentioned 'in the old Greenhouse Garden a Phesentry with a leanto Ruff on...', commenting that some slates (from the 'Ruff') had been damaged in a storm. Sale particulars in the same year also noted a pheasant house. Perhaps the 'two lemon trees, orange trees, oleanders, a datura and a guava in tubs' also mentioned, were overwintered in the shelter of the greenhouse/conservatory. By 1865 the OS map shows the Harveys had removed the glasshouse from this garden, and had created a new path through the garden, previously entered only from the east. Perhaps it was around this time that a niche or alcove was built into the rear wall. In the twentieth century a wooden arbour was built around the alcove and is now being replaced, and lost views towards the water opened up again.

Archaeologists from Exeter Archaeology have completed a survey of the Camellia Garden and done some digging. The far doorway was created in the perimeter wall only in the nineteenth century. They also dated part of the retaining wall as having been built in the reign of Elizabeth I, long before anyone had heard of camellias. It is well known that John Gilbert used prisoners of war from the Spanish Armada 'in the levelling of his grounds', and this is one of the places where they were employed.

Eloquent in his plant lists and descriptions, S. Wyndham Fitzherbert added to the nomenclature confusion. He described the spot as the 'Battery-garden' in his *Gardeners' Chronicle* article of 16 March 1901:

In the 'Battery-garden,' that doubtless owes its name to the spot having been fortified during the wars of the commonwealth, when Dartmouth and Kingswear were the scene of a protracted struggle, grows a fine tree of *Gevuina avellana*, a native of Chile, 20ft [6m] in height...and a wall some 10ft [3m] high is bountifully draped with *Trachelospermum jasminoides* whose growth are thickly starred in August days with a wealth of white, deliciously scented flowers. Hard by *Berberidopsis corallina* bears its racemes of drooping crimson flowers as late as November...

These are plants growing in the Camellia Garden. Fitzherbert was describing this space, but calling it by another name, and attributing its construction to the wrong period. (The real 'battery' lower down the slope, complete with two cannon, probably dates from the Napoleonic wars.) Battery Garden, too, is the location noted by twentieth-century owners. Charles Williams, who kept a Planting Book between 1916 and 1920, noted two *Corylopsis* species (*paniculata* and *pauciflora*) near the Battery Garden path as well as two camellias and *Magnolia stellata* in the garden itself. Max Mallowan's Planting Book from 1941 to 1971 refers just a couple of times to the Camellia Garden.

So the name may be a relatively new one, applied to the garden with the hindsight of history. It is appropriate. It is fitting that some of the camellias in the garden may survive from the original planting. It is fitting, too, that today's visitors, newcomers, 'strangers' (as William Dean of Croome Park would say), should have some signposting to the significance of the little walled enclosure. Here both the history of the site and the plant enthusiast's perspective come into focus.

In 2003 archaeologists from Exeter Archaeology did some digging in this area. Their uncovering of the remains of the workings of the system that two hundred years ago provided heat for plants that didn't actually need it is something for specialists to puzzle endlessly over. They also dug up fragments of clay pots and a Prince of Wales clay pipe, and found a pretty pebbled floor in the arbour.

Most importantly, they discovered that behind the wall that we see today are remnants of a much older wall. Local lore tells that the walls

Part of the recently excavated brick flue that ran in steps up the west wall and turned to heat the rear wall of the Camellia House.

of this garden were built by prisoners-of-war from the Spanish Armada. This is now confirmed by archaeologists. Across the centuries we find that another piece of the jigsaw fits into place.

There are further complications in the rough stone walling that surrounds the garden's other sides. If you have a mind to it, you can try puzzling out the different building sequences. Reading the stones in a wall is like reading the leaves of a tree: aficionados can get deeply into the details. The instincts of the plant twitcher with a desire to identify unusual specimens are not unlike those of the archaeologist.

The back or north wall is a retaining wall, built into the hillside, and in the past had a glazed building against it. The wall was once heated by hot air, in the days when gardeners thought exotic evergreens like camellias and Portugal laurel were not hardy and needed winter protection. There seems to have been a furnace or stove below ground on the right or south-east corner, and hot air would have risen in a substantial brick-lined flue built in a stepped pattern towards the back wall. Rising diagonally from right to left across the back wall, from the right-hand side, is a continuation of the brick-lined flue.

If this is a hot-air flue, to heat the camellia wall, it is distinctly unusual. Everyone knows warm air rises, and it's best to begin heating a wall low down, but one would normally expect such a flue to travel the length of the wall at the same height and then make a U-turn to cross the wall higher up. Providing heat for susceptible plants was a kind of competition by the time this garden took its current shape: the latest technology was available through publications like Miller's *Dictionary* and its successors.

The Luxuriant Legacy of Father Kemel

The Quakers quietly gardened and grew plants at home. The Society of Jesus, however, was formed as a mission, and incidentally recorded and discovered plants as they travelled in their quest to discover and save souls. Georg Josef Kemel (1661–1706) was a Moravian Jesuit whose mission was to botanize and proselytize the island of Luzon in

You can get bogged down in plant identification and archaeological puzzles and fail to see the wood for the trees. It's important occasionally to raise your eyes to the wider landscape to keep things in perspective. One of the gardening jobs at Greenway is to open out views, like the one from the Camellia Garden arbour.

Camellia blooms vary from simple species like this *Camellia sasanqua* (above) to an astonishing range of double forms. Breeding new cultivars is a world-wide passion, matched only by taxonomic disputes about identification.

the Philippines – the sole Asiatic region where substantial numbers of native inhabitants were successfully converted to Christianity. Father Kemel himself never saw a camellia, but some decades after his death Carl von Linné or Linnaeus named the new plant in his honour in 1753. (We should remember that common names don't count in international currency. Just as vernacular plant names got latinized, so did people – hence Linnaeus, Camellus, Lobelius and many others.)

The first camellias to arrive in Britain in the 1730s were from Japan – *Camellia japonica*. The handsome glossy leaves and beautiful winter flowers made them instantly popular. The plantsmen and gardeners who grew the early introductions found the plants so striking that they assumed at first that they needed winter protection, and grew them under glass, in heated buildings. (You still find old glasshouses in old gardens growing old camellias.) Some of the camellias in Greenway's Camellia Garden may first have grown in its early glasshouse.

They say a camel is like an animal designed by a committee. The camellia, on the other hand, is a flower that improved when a few extra hands came on board. From the beginning camellias impressed plant collectors with their beautiful leaves, but their flowers were the real bonus, especially because they appear in winter. The learning curve in camellia cultivation included providing the right soil conditions. Chris Beardshaw reminds us that, like rhododendrons and the Ericaceae, camellias need acidic soil. Greenway is basically alkaline, and plantsman owners have had to import peaty soil over the last century or so to accommodate their treasured specimens.

Many other camellia species were introduced after *Camellia japonica*, but hybrids were unknown. Then, some time around 1917, the plant collector George Forrest sent home seeds of *Camellia saluenensis* from the Salween river area in Yunnan, China. J. C. Williams (who was about to become father-in-law of Mary Bolitho of Greenway) crossed one of its pink-flowered seedlings with pollen from a white-flowered *C. japonica*. The hybrids that resulted at Caerhays embodied the best merits of both parents. *C.* x *williamsii* cultivars are hardy, flower profusely and have the decency to drop their spent blooms rather than keeping the browning petals on the branches to sour the colour effect of pure icing-sugar pinks and whites amid glossy green leaves. There has been no stopping the hybridizers. Today there are nearly 40,000 named varieties of camellia.

Greenway's Horticultural Heritage

Greenway's plant wealth was first brought to life at precisely the turn of the century by the effusive descriptions of S. Wyndham Fitzherbert in *The Garden* and the *Gardeners' Chronicle*. (The author did not ignore the setting, and described the steep drop to the ever-fascinating river in poetic prose.) The property was then in the ownership of Thomas Bedford Bolitho, MP for St Ives, who divided his time between Greenway and his Cornish home, Trewidden, near Penzance. Bolitho was an enthusiastic plantsman. Descriptions of Trewidden make a fitting parallel for Greenway: 'There has never been any attempt to make this garden a collection of great numbers of plants, but rather to grow some of the best shrubs, and try to get these to grow into natural and beautiful plants,' wrote Charles Williams.

When Bolitho died in 1919 his daughter Mary and her husband Charles Williams, MP for Tavistock and Torquay, moved to Greenway.

Below The layered mature conifer in this view towards the river from a point to the east of the house is a variety of Japanese cedar, *Cryptomeria japonica* var. *sinensis*, probably planted *c.* 1850–80 by Bolitho. The fork in the path is not far from the point where the iron fence in the cartouche on page 128 disappears uphill – illustrating Greenway's change from a 'picturesque' layout to a wooded plantsman's garden.

A sheltered raised area to the east of the Walled Garden catches the setting sun. Agatha Christie used it for evening entertainment, laying out a putting green on the lawn. The rear border contains choice shrubs, including the orange-flowered *Abutilon megapotamicum* and *Itea ilicifolia* with drooping catkin-like seedheads

Helpfully for the archives, Charles and Mary Williams listed the plants they found growing at Greenway when they arrived, and kept a record of their own extensive plantings. (Charles Williams even returned after the war to help the new owners identify what was there.) Plantsman pedigree is clearly significant. As the son of J. C. Williams of Caerhays Castle, Charles Williams had inherited some of his horticultural and hybridizing genes.

Once established at Greenway, the tradition of plantsmanship and plant collecting – if not plant breeding – persisted through the twentieth century. Charles Williams added many rhododendrons and magnolias as well as other choice shrubs, making the garden yet more colourful and varied, before deciding to move back to Caerhays in the mid 1930s. Once more Greenway was sold twice in quick succession, in 1937 and 1938. According to sales particulars of the time, 'The house stands within gardens and grounds of exceptional attraction, enriched with sub-tropical shrubs and specimen trees of great variety. In addition there are two magnificent walled gardens containing Vineries, Peach houses, various further glasshouses and other buildings…'

This time the denouement was a happy one. The house and some 32 acres was purchased by Mrs Max Mallowan, wife of the distinguished archaeologist who had worked at Nineveh and Ur of the Chaldees, and otherwise known as the distinguished murder-mystery writer Agatha Christie. Apart from the war years, Greenway has remained in the family ever since, in the hands of her son-in-law and daughter, Anthony and Rosalind Hicks, and their son Matthew Prichard.

Agatha Christie had been brought up in Torquay, and in her autobiography noted that she had called as a child with her mother at Greenway – 'a house that my mother had always said, and I had thought also, was the most perfect of the various properties on the Dart'. Neither Professor Mallowan nor Agatha Christie was an experienced gardener, but both loved the garden and took an active interest in the planting. Max Mallowan started a Garden Book in 1941 to note the camellias, magnolias and other shrubs he planted. During World War II Greenway was at first used as a nursery for evacuated children. (The walled gardens then later became a nursery for plants!) In 1943 the house was requisitioned as the officers' mess for the 10th Flotilla of US patrol boats preparing on the Dart for the invasion of France.

Greenway Nursery was begun by Agatha Christie in 1947 and ran till the end of the century in the walled garden. It specialized in rare and interesting plants propagated on site (they sold almost a hundred varieties of camellia), and some of the shrubs remaining in the garden borders are stock plants.

Agatha Christie had visited Greenway as a child and was delighted when the property came on the market in 1938.

Hydrangeas have been favourites of a number of Greenway's gardening owners. This one is the choice *Hydrangea macrophylla* 'Nigra'.

The complex of 'useful' garden areas to the north of the house have variously served as nursery, tennis court, kitchen garden and frame yards. You make your way through this area via a series of intriguing doorways through walls covered with rampant choice climbers and shrubs.

The existence of the nursery ensured that the rarer and more tender plants in the garden were constantly replenished. In addition, Anthony Hicks built up an extensive collection of southern hemisphere trees and shrubs, concentrating on magnolias, camellias, michelias, eucryphias and nothofagus and customers to the nursery were sometimes invited to visit the garden.

Greenway now welcomes the public far more often – from March (Christie's favourite time of year at Greenway) to October. Gardener Nick Howarth describes the challenge faced by the National Trust as 'keeping the garden looking as if it is poised on the edge of wildness'. Only a visit will tell you how well it is succeeding in this magical place poised on the edge of the river Dart.

BOVERIDGE HOUSE
Guess Who Invited Miss Jekyll?

Whole villages are hidden in the dents and wrinkles of Dorset's topography. Roadside houses and cottages hide behind tall hedge banks, only the odd nameplate or mailbox by a gate giving away their whereabouts. Graft into this natural concealment the picturesque tradition by which the grander landlords of past centuries manipulated the approach to their dwellings to create a sense of anticipation and awe in their visitors, and you'll find a house like Boveridge hard to find indeed. Once someone has told you the precise way to the entrance gates you wend a long winding way between open parkland and concealing trees before encountering the calculated surprise turning into the carriage circle between the house's porte cochère and the ornate stable block.

It's a pilgrimage that only the privileged can make, because visitors are welcomed only on special open days. Many local people don't even know where it is – or that it's there at all. Until recently this category included Alison Smith, Boveridge's enthusiastic gardener, whose inspiring hands are gradually coaxing the precious garden shapes back into view. She grew up locally, quite unaware of its existence. She was working in the famous gardens of Tresco and returned to Dorset to continue her horticultural studies when she heard there was 'a little-known Jekyll garden' on her doorstep. For a dedicated gardener this was an opportunity not to be missed. Alison came along to offer her services voluntarily, and after a short while she was given a job.

Losing gardens has become less easy nowadays, particularly Jekyll gardens. In Gertrude Jekyll's home county of Surrey, the number of gardens claiming to be of her making are as numerous as pieces of the True Cross: there are far too many for them all possibly to be authentic. We have come a long way from the time when the American garden designer Beatrix Farrand had the foresight to rescue Jekyll's plans from the wastepaper basket and send them to the Reef Point Gardens Collection at the University of California for safekeeping.

Boveridge appears in the lists of gardens planted by Jekyll, but for some reason and for some time nobody paid it much attention.

An Outline of the Plot

The hiddenness of Boveridge is partly intentional. The property is leased to an educational institution that must retain its privacy. Boveridge House School was founded by Miss Peggie Harper in 1966. The management of the school changed on her retirement in 1998, and its name was changed to the Philip Green Memorial School, reflecting the involvement of the trust of that name in its redevelopment. The school caters for boarding and day pupils aged between nine and nineteen who have learning difficulties, speech and language problems, and associated emotional vulnerability. Gardens are often lyrically described as a haven, a retreat or an oasis; and in the case of Boveridge the isolation is not just a figure of speech, but a necessary part of providing the students and staff with protection and security.

The school opens the gardens to the public on just a handful of occasions during the holidays for fundraising events, at the same time as other gardens in the Cranborne area. Public access is not allowed otherwise. To date the cost of caring for the gardens and reinstating the original planting in discrete areas has been raised by the school's trustees and the enterprising head teacher, Lesley Walter. Chris Beardshaw has been lending a hand and discussing the feasibility of further restoration. Now a bid to seek major funding for other parts of the garden is to be launched.

Boveridge House was originally built in about 1800 by Henry Brunker. Nearly two centuries later it was registered by English Heritage as a Grade II garden because of the merits of its formal and water gardens dating from the 1920s; it had emerged that the layout was designed by Thomas Mawson and the planting planned by Gertrude Jekyll. During the first half of the twentieth century, the gardens were maintained by the Gordon family with a dozen or so gardeners. Even members of the Gordon family, however, seem to have been unaware that Gertrude Jekyll had ever been involved in the garden's creation: they thought that the garden was entirely the work of Mrs Charles Gordon.

When the weather vane on Boveridge House points from south-east to south-west, it points towards gardens designed by Edward Mawson.

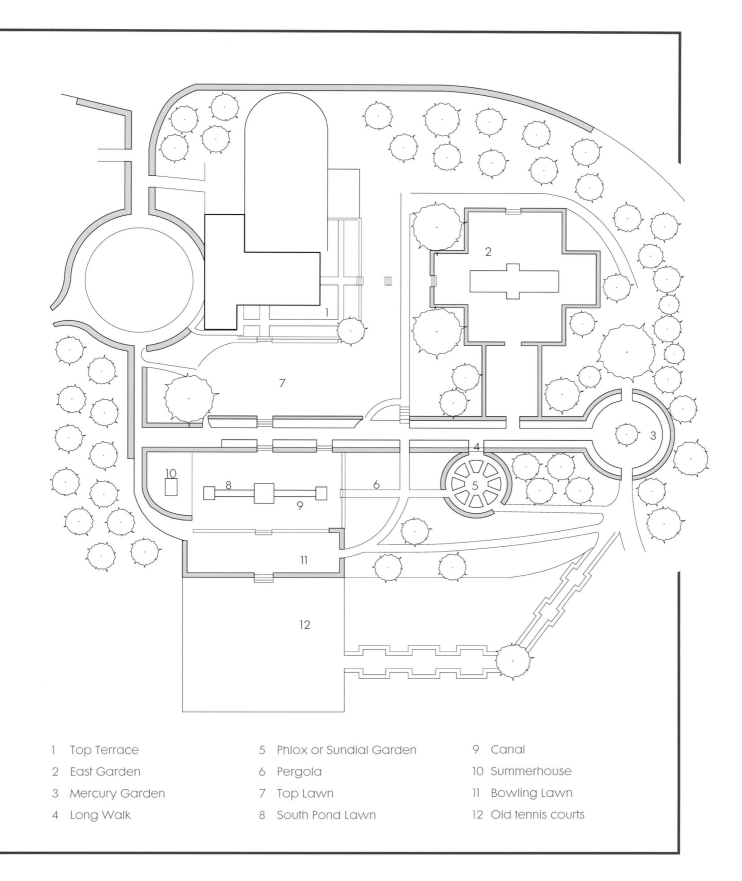

1 Top Terrace
2 East Garden
3 Mercury Garden
4 Long Walk
5 Phlox or Sundial Garden
6 Pergola
7 Top Lawn
8 South Pond Lawn
9 Canal
10 Summerhouse
11 Bowling Lawn
12 Old tennis courts

'Do you know you've got a Jekyll garden here?' someone asked. The trustees of the school to which Boveridge is now home wanted to know more. They sent for copies of the planting plans and the plant lists and became ever more fascinated. Then it gradually emerged that the garden had been laid out not by Lutyens, Jekyll's usual partner, but by Thomas Mawson. A Mawson-Jekyll collaboration was hitherto unheard of. So how did it come about?

Garden Partnerships

The new English landscape garden style – like Capability Brown's at Croome Park – had swept the western world in the eighteenth century. (Georgian Boveridge struck Mawson on first sight as typical of this

When Boveridge was new, around 1800, the 'countryside' would have swept up to the very doors of the house. The early twentieth century preferred a gradation from formality and artifice in the foreground to greater naturalism as garden dissolved into landscape, as this view from the roof towards the south-east demonstrates.

style.) A second flowering of Englishness happened in the decades on either side of the year 1900, when Arts and Crafts ideas merged with imaginative, if eclectic, architecture in a way that gave plants their due place in the garden composition. It was a glorious marriage of living plants and handsome structures that allowed a house to be linked to its setting – as we see at Boveridge. Many scholars have written many reams on the collaborations and rivalries between gardeners and architects of the period, the merits of classicism and the vernacular, hardy plants versus bedding and so on. Here we shall need to meet a handful of the protagonists.

Architecture softened by planting was the keynote of the great English garden designers of the early twentieth century. This summerhouse at Boveridge evokes those fabled Edwardian 'gardens of a golden afternoon'.

If Bridge End Garden might merit a small blue 'Jekyll Was Here' plaque (see page 64), Boveridge's claim is far greater: Gertrude Jekyll certainly designed the planting here. The plans exist, scrawled with her inimitable inky drifts of plant names. Also extant is the small black notebook she compiled to accompany the plans. Its feint-ruled pages show how businesslike the talented plantswoman was – after all, she ran a nursery at Munstead Wood in Surrey. Area by area and bed by bed the required numbers of plants are listed and priced. Later annotation in red crayon records the despatch of the plants.

'A Jekyll garden', the essential companion to the Lutyens house had almost been forgotten until the reputation of Gertrude Jekyll was rescued in the 1980s by a handful of gardeners and scholars. The 'Jekyll-Lutyens partnership' is familiar to gardeners; (architects may prefer references to a 'Lutyens-Jekyll design') and a byword for all that was most desirable in the late Victorian and Edwardian country residence. But Jekyll-Mawson? The pairing is unheard of. But here, at Boveridge House, it happened. The simple answer is that it was not exactly a collaboration: first Mawson planned the layout and then Jekyll designed the planting.

By 1920 Thomas Hayton Mawson (1861–1933) had earned an international reputation and had offices in Lancaster, London, Vancouver and Athens. A landmark in his career in Britain was the publication in 1900 of *The Art and Craft of Garden Making*. The book expressed the fruits of his experience in designing both country-house gardens and public parks, and served as an eloquent advertisement for his belief that architecture and landscape architecture should relate to one another. He thought that there should be a sound relationship between house and garden on the one hand and house and landscape on the other, and laid great emphasis on successfully blending the architectural and horticultural. For the child of a Lancashire cotton warper who left school at twelve and was largely self-taught, this was not bad going. 'His secret was to spend all available time reading any books he could lay his hands on and visiting successful schemes within reach,' wrote his grandson David Mawson.

Gertrude Jekyll was seventy-seven in 1920, when she designed the planting for 'Boveridge Park', and when she was painted by William Nicholson.

Members of the establishment sometimes looked down on the self-made Mawson and quarrelled with the concept he called 'landscape architecture'. He incurred the scorn of the fiery William Robinson: 'Many, not satisfied with the good word "Landscape gardener" used by Loudon, Repton and many other excellent men, call themselves "Landscape Architects" – a stupid term of French origin implying the union of two absolutely distinct studies.'

Time has assured the pedigree of the term landscape architect. Garden designs like that of Boveridge and many urban park and town planning schemes have placed Mawson's name alongside that of Edwin Lutyens in the ranks of great garden-makers.

Friction at New Place

Mawson and Lutyens first rubbed shoulders on a completely different project some years earlier, in 1907. In his autobiography Mawson recalled that Mrs Franklyn of Botley in Hampshire asked him to advise her on a garden layout for New Place, the house that Edwin Lutyens was building for her son. Mawson demurred: '"Surely, with Mr. Lutyens," I said, "you don't need anyone to design the gardens." "Well, the fact is we wish you to do them, and Mr. Lutyens knows this and understands."'

In fact, Lutyens had already contacted Miss Jekyll about the New Place project in 1906. Already by this time she seldom travelled beyond the range of her own pony-cart. When designing a scheme she requested a thorough briefing about the site and was able to rely on her own experience to advise on planting. Lutyens sent her his sketched plan of house and grounds with a list of suggestions and questions in the characteristic abbreviated language they had developed for such exchanges. Some answers appear to have been forthcoming, because Lutyens's sketch exists with later amendments.

Thomas Mawson was the first great English landscape architect. He was commissioned to design the garden layout at Boveridge in 1920 by Charles Gorden.

Jane Brown in *Gardens of a Golden Afternoon,* supposes that Lutyens must have visited Munstead to finish the scheme. However, she notes that 'there is no record of further letters' and – more tellingly – comments that the surviving garden was disappointing: 'I do not think either the summer houses or the formal garden were even constructed, and the rest of the layout is now much altered.'

Perhaps the reason for that disappointment is that Mrs Franklyn put the New Place garden design firmly into Mawson's hands. A certain amount of gentlemanly feinting took place. Mawson insisted on meeting Lutyens to make sure he agreed on the collaboration, to find that 'in the kindest way possible he assured me that if he was not allowed to design the garden, there was no one he would rather co-operate with than me'. In retrospect Mawson too was disappointed and in his autobiography twenty years later felt that it had been a mistake: 'I am certain that Lutyens without me would have achieved a greater success; and, on the other hand, I am sure that I could have done a much finer garden had I been left entirely untrammelled. My partial failure resulted from my attempts to interpret Lutyens in the garden, he having one set of conventions and I another.'

'My clients I soon discovered were keenly interested in their gardens.'

Thomas Mawson

What Lutyens felt about New Place is not recorded. Next year, in April 1908, he felt distinct nervousness at the prospect of having to make a formal reply to an opening speech by Mawson before the Architectural Association. The discussion was about the natural versus the formal in garden design. While Mawson was a seasoned lecturer, Lutyens was unaccustomed to public speaking and had the instinctual pragmatist's dislike of theorizing. He sought the advice of Miss Jekyll and some of her ideas echoed in his phrasing. 'A garden scheme should have a backbone, a central idea beautifully phrased.' He deplored gardens that were 'merely a collection of features' and argued on the importance of relating 'every wall, path, stone and flower bed' to the central idea. He accorded prominence to plants: 'The true adornment of a garden lies surely in its flowers and plants,' but added a note of warning: 'No artist has so wide a palette as the garden designer; no artist has more need of both discretion and reserve.' The speech went down well, to his relief, and he spent a happy afternoon with Miss Jekyll afterwards.

The Boveridge Commission

For some years the rivals went their separate, successful ways. The peaceful days of Edwardian opulence were succeeded by the horrors of World War I, which deprived many a country house of both its heirs and its workforce, but still some grand houses were built and some gardens made. As life picked up (where it could) post-war, Mawson's firm received two commissions from 'well-known shipowners' in early 1920. One of them, Boveridge Park, had been purchased by Charles W. Gordon in 1909 and was being refurbished by the architect Guy Dawber (1861–1938), known to some circles as 'the Lutyens of the West Country'. Mawson's first impression of Boveridge was of a 'large and somewhat austere' Georgian house in a parkland setting suggesting to him the work of Capability Brown or Repton.

Mawson's response was typical of his way of borrowing the rules of architecture to relate a building to its surroundings.

This Victorian view of 1866 towards the south-east façade of the house shows an intervening stage in the evolution of the garden. With its panels of bedding plants stranded in the middle of a vast lawn, making an isolated garden feature that bears no relation to the building, it embodies all that Thomas Mawson deplored in garden style.

There was already an extensive garden in the formal manner, replete
with a fountain, court, and grass glades bordered by cypress hedges.
There was a terrace on the east side some distance from the house,
but none of these features seemed to have any relation to the building,
which called for a response in the garden, and especially on the south
side, where the park views are the most extensive.

Mawson liked to echo the geometry of a house by creating terraces or
level platforms leading outwards from the principal façades. Terraces
would be wide or narrow depending upon the steepness of the slope,
and linked by stone steps set into hedged banks or walls. All classical
garden design depends on making the most of a main axis or vista
looking from the house, and on what Mawson called the 'east' side of
the house (which strictly speaking faces south-east) this was carried
over the long rectangle of the lily-pond. On the 'southern' elevation he
designed a more complex series of stepped levels, as he described:

On the east side we confined our plans to the limits and levels of the original garden, but on the south the gardens were projected far into the park by way of a series of terraces of varying depth and width. First there is the stone terraces next to the house, then a grass terrace supported by a wall filled with Alpine flowers, followed by a terrace eight feet [2.4m] lower, laid out with panels of rose beds and a central canal for water lilies and other hardy aquatic plants.'

The long, narrow canal was a favourite Mawson device. It stretches along the narrow terrace at right angles to the main vista, interrupting your progress out into the landscape and forcing you to look to right and left along the terrace and to appreciate what Mawson termed the cross-axis. Now in need of repair, the canal is one of the features we find Chris Beardshaw and Alison Smith setting to work on.

'Below this again, there is a green bowling alley, and finally an expanse of lawn large enough for several tennis courts,' Mawson wrote.

Tennis courts were indeed built on the lawn and for some years the five Gordon daughters played set and match with other bright young things, but all have long since faded out of the picture.

The progression from house to parkland embodied the classic transition from artifice and built structures to the living green of grass and yew hedges bordering the open ground dotted with clumps of trees and grazing horses. In both directions, from the house south outwards to the park and back from the park towards the house, the pace is measured and the views are directed and controlled. None of it is unduly ostentatious. Each element seems to reflect the simplicity of the house and anchor it in the landscape.

Perhaps Mawson was never intended to undertake the major part of the planting, apart from some rose beds. After describing his layout in his autobiography, he makes a few general remarks about the merits and constraints of gardening on chalk. Acid-loving shrubs of the Ericaceae, obviously, were excluded, but roses and 'nearly every known deciduous shrub grow vigorously, as do most of the conifers, evergreen oak, and holly'. He concludes his account of his work at Boveridge with a note of commiseration on the laborious nature of a chalk soil for construction and gardening alike. He must have kept his eye on progress, however, for a few years later, in 1927, he could write that his keen clients had 'continued to improve the quality of the soil and the lawns, which proves once more that gardens grow for those who love them'. And for gardeners who work hard on them, gardener Alison would add, thinking of all the organic matter that the chalk soil can gobble up.

Is it significant that Mawson referred to 'the soil and the lawns' and not – apart from mentioning roses – to the planting, which must surely have been glorious by 1927? Would it be over-suspicious to detect a note of sour grapes? Miss Jekyll had been called in to complete the picture for which he had set up the frame. Mawson was a fine plantsman. He had done his groundwork in horticulture as well as architecture and had been a partner in the Mawson Brothers Lakeland Nurseries, where he carried out the design work while his brothers ran the nursery. But for some reason that no one has yet fathomed, the celebrated Miss Jekyll, not Mawson, was commissioned to design the planting of the borders in the new Boveridge gardens, and design the borders is what she did.

Someone has ventured the suggestion that the commission was kept hush-hush because Mrs Charles Gordon didn't want Mr Charles Gordon to know how much she was spending on planting her garden. The division of labour seems plausible: the men did the architecture bit and the ladies fussed about the flowers. Was there conscious concealment, or has time (when gardens were considered unimportant) merely blurred memory and effaced documentary evidence? At the moment we know of no motives. We merely know the facts.

Hubs of Change

Towards the southern tip of the garden, as kempt lawn and straight lines soften into shrubberies and bosky informality, the layout features two or three circular clearings, in plan looking like cogs in a machine linked by shafts. They make pivotal points in a tour of the garden, where the axis of a path shifts and the visitor (like the 'stranger' William Dean envisaged visiting Croome Park, page 41) is obliged by the design to change direction. Gertrude Jekyll described this as the sort of spot where 'paths meet and swing round in a circle. There may be some accentuating ornament – a sundial, a stone vase for flowers, or a tank for a...water-lily.' Two such spaces at Boveridge are the Mercury Pool Garden and the Sundial Garden, both of which have been the subject of recent restoration projects.

In the Mercury Garden the pond was full of earth and plants rather than water so it had to be emptied, repaired and resealed. Alison Smith replanted a circle of yew hedging. Mercury himself had gone missing way back in the 1950s when the Gordon family sold up. In fact, he flew off to the United States with a member of the family, and lives there still. So there began a search for a figure to pose on his empty plinth, and the funding for its reinstatement. The figure that forms the centrepiece in the canal was made by the firm of Crowthers, who have been casting statues since 1908. It turned out they were able

'The chances of securing an interesting garden on chalk are equal to those on almost any other soil, but no other garden is as trying to the men who construct it, as a garden on a chalky base, especially if the chalk be wet.'

Thomas Mawson

to supply a replacement Winged Mercury, quite probably from the original mould. The John Spedan Lewis Foundation generously donated the funding to purchase and install the statue.

According to the Jekyll plans, the original Mercury Garden had a series of curving beds containing the usual herbaceous mixture of acanthus, delphiniums and other classy perennials, plus generous helpings of various irises. One day these beds will be reinstated, too – once the ground elder has been eradicated. In the meantime the clean surfaces of yew, grass, stone and water are pleasing to modern eyes.

The Sundial Garden is the second 'hub' to be the subject of restoration. At some time in the not-too-distant past, perhaps in the 1970s, the overgrown yew hedges surrounding it were replaced with a circle of vertical wooden posts by the then head gardener. Climbing roses were planted to swarm up the pillars and festoon the swags of rope overhead. The central area up to the sundial base was grassed over. The feature may have worked for a while, but by Alison's day the rope had rotted, the uprights looked all too much like naked telegraph poles, and only where the roses rose above deer-grazing level could any leaves or flowers survive. It was time for a makeover, and fortunately by now Jekyll's original plans and plantings had come to light.

So far this project scores full marks on both the 'restoration' and 're-construction' criteria Sylvia Landsberg set out (see page 23). It was just possible to 'read' in the grass a few indications that a symmetrical arrangement of beds had once surrounded the central sundial. Turf is a well-established forensic focus for garden detectives. Well before garden restoration became commonplace, long, dry summers would turn areas of uninterrupted lawn into a patchwork of browns and greens, revealing to the unsuspecting observer that gardens, too, had history. Famously, the shapes of formal beds, grassed over in the past on grounds of style or economy, gradually became evident as patches of deeper green within surrounding parched grass. (Both Jacobean and Victorian lost gardens have been rediscovered in this way.) Sometimes, as at Boveridge, faint dips and irregularities in the surface level are detectable. In other cases, differences in vegetation act as clues, with variations in the broadleaved 'weeds' of lawns signalling panels where the soil was once deep-dug for bedding plants in contrast with areas of poorer soil always covered by turf or by gravel paths that have been grassed over.

The Boveridge masterplan just showed a hedged circular garden space with central sundial. The detailed plan, however, is subtitled 'Phlox Garden' in Jekyll's hand. It showed eight trapezoid beds radiating from the eight faces of the octagonal sundial base. 'Typical of the 1920s,' comments Chris Beardshaw. The planting was simple and low-key: the centres of the segmental beds featured alternating pairs of phlox cultivars in two-colour combinations. They were framed by a classical Jekyll pairing of two plants we now know as *Aster divaricatus* and *Bergenia cordifolia*. 'There is a small-growing perennial Aster, *A. corymbosus*, from a foot to eighteen inches [30-45cm] high, that seems to enjoy close association with other plants and is easy to grow anywhere.' Miss Jekyll found it, 'in conjunction with Megasea, one of the most useful of those filling plants for edge spaces that just want some pretty trimming but are not wide enough for anything larger'. The evergreen megasea or bergenia pleased her at the edges of beds and borders because: 'It seems desirable to have, next the grass, some foliage of rather distinct and important size or form.'

The handwriting on Gertrude Jekyll's plans is unmistakeable. This detailed plan is labelled first 'Sundial Garden' and then 'Phlox Garden'.

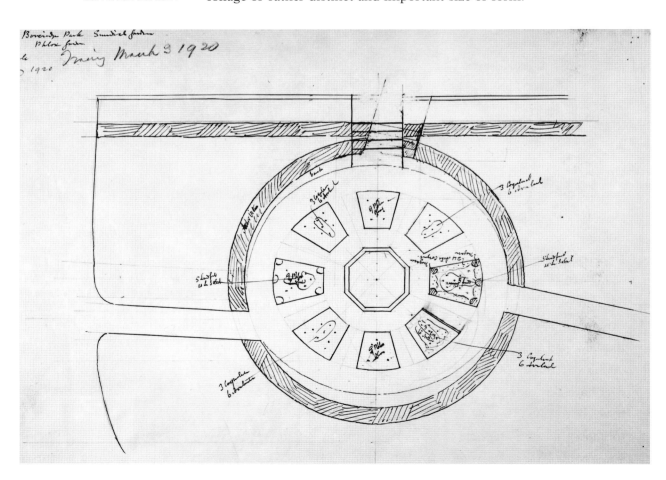

To restore this part of the garden to the master plan, Alison drew out the geometrical beds and dug them over, incorporating tons of soil conditioner to improve the hungry chalky earth. She also prepared the circular band of ground where the new yew hedge would go. When it came to planting day there was a surprise for onlookers. All the young yew trees were festooned like small Christmas trees, each with a little tied-on parcel. Close inspection showed it to be scented soap – Imperial Leather, to be precise. 'It's to deter the deer,' said Alison. (This would surely have amused Lord Leverhulme of Port Sunlight, pal and patron of Thomas Mawson.) The deterrent is a suggestion from one of Alison's friends. Alison explained that when she planted the yew hedge around the Mercury Garden earlier in the year, the young yew trees were promptly hard-pruned by deer. The Cranborne deer have a discriminating palate: they like roses, baby yew and hollyhocks but – unlike the Hestercombe deer, who also have a Jekyll menu to choose from – don't relish sedums. So the parcels on the young yews symbolize the fruits of experience.

New planting naturally has a raw, bitty look for a year or two, especially until individual hedging plants bind together into a whole. Kept well nourished, yew grows faster than most people realize and in a few years' time this hedge will create an enclosed flower garden.

Plants of bergenia – the children appreciate their common name of elephant's ears – and *Aster divaricatus* were easy to come by. Jekyll's original *Phlox paniculata* cultivars were more of a problem to source. Jekyll specified 'Rosebud', 'Le Soleil' and 'Lindfield'. Alison used 'Orange Perfection', 'White Admiral', 'Judy' and 'Rembrandt' as the nearest available match. It is hoped that original varieties can be sourced and propagated in the next few years to replace the substitutes.

With the sundial base and plinth cleaned up, rebuilt and good as new, the garden must look as it originally did when first planted, way back in the early 1920s. Today it's not gramophone records of the Charleston you might faintly hear emanating from the open windows of the house, but sounds of an altogether more frantic tempo as the Boveridge students express their up-to-the-minute tastes. Under Alison's care the yews won't take long to blur into a continuous hedge, and then the visitor will once again come upon an enclosed gem of a garden, giving them pause to stop and enjoy the sight.

Gumshoe Detectives

Stone-edged canals were typically architectural features in gardens of the early 1900s. Mawson used them to emphasize the strong axial lines of his layouts. At Boveridge the canal interrupts your stepped descent to the south-west, theoretically making you turn to left or right to walk along the terrace, although in fact inconspicuous stepping stones amid the jostling water-lily leaves permit a slightly undignified short cut on either side of the centrepiece.

The low water level means there's a leak somewhere: the canal will have to be drained, rendered and sealed. First some homework has to be done on those water lilies. The theory part is getting them identified. The practical is to take cuttings for the now lily-less Mercury pool, plus stock plants for replacing in the canal once it is mended. The exercise seems to epitomize what gardening is all about: you could call it a marriage of scholarship and slime. On the one hand we have the neat conventions of botany, with their structured patterns of Latin genus and species, and on the other an all-to-real world of jumbled roots tangling in soil and water. Observation backed by knowledge is the connection. The work in the pond that Alison and Chris undertake epitomizes what garden restoration is about, too. You need the experts on hand with the filed references and the microscopes and the names, but you also need perceptive educated hands-on people in the field with enough nous to consider and to record what they encounter before they proceed with any course of action. It's the best kind of oversize gumshoe detective work. Alison Smith and Chris Beardshaw relish the challenge.

Alison and Chris find three different kinds of water lily in the canal; a fourth was found in the east pond. All are identified by an expert and turn out to be varieties known to Gertrude Jekyll. Among them are two hybrids from the celebrated French Latour-Marliac

This axial view towards the south-west façade of the house from the far side of the canal illustrates Mawson's stepped, architectural approach. Chris Beardshaw has other things on his mind.

nursery, which produced the very first pink water lily cultivar in 1879. Their names, 'Marliacea Albida' (described by Jekyll as 'difficult to surpass') and 'Marliacea Carnea', helpfully describe their tones of white and deep flesh-pink. Another water lily, the white *Nymphaea tuberosa* 'Maxima', is known to be strong-growing and vigorous: would Jekyll have prescribed it for a confined space? *Nymphaea* 'Froebelii', with small, single, wine-red flowers, was new and relatively unknown to Jekyll at the turn of the century but has long been established as garden-worthy. She would have been glad to be able to commend it.

The canal garden once had rose beds cluttering its lawns. These don't appear in the grand Jekyll plan; presumably they were Mawson's. He mentioned them in his description, and they are still present in a photograph from around 1950. Since roses really don't enjoy Boveridge's chalky soil, some of us might suggest that the lost rose beds might be allowed to rest in peace.

Once again, the complexities of the restoration question raise their heads. Because the rose beds were once planned and planted, must they be reinstated? Even in a garden like Boveridge, created by known garden-makers in a narrow timespan, there is room for debate, and many voices will want to have their say. But that is another story.

The task in hand is to extricate a good stock of water lilies from the canal pool before it is drained for repair, and to identify the varieties. Gardener Alison Smith is interested to find that all the lilies are those originally planted, including *Nymphaea* 'Marliacea Carnea'.

A Border Campaign

The long border planted the length of Mawson's second 'grass terrace' looks glorious in late summer. Jekyll's faithful perennials like achillea, echinops and sedum, penstemon, purple sage and verbascum weave together in dreamy drifts, attracting butterflies and bees. Some of the most eye-catching plants, however, are different forms of the old honeywort, *Cerinthe major*, and the tall 'wire-stemmed' pale purple plates of *Verbena bonariensis*, defying the graded border profile by soaring above their neighbours. You don't find these on Miss Jekyll's plant lists: they're plants of the moment, plants of today. They look wonderful in her border: surely she would have approved? But – if restoration with official funding were to be sought – would such plants be banned as 'inauthentic'?

Why change anything? Alas, hidden and unnoticed among the robust summer survivors flowering at waist height lurks that pernicious scourge of old gardens, ground elder. The border is full of it. It infiltrates the roots of handsome mature shrubs as well as herbaceous perennials. Eradicating it would be an excruciating task: in the case of perennials, best to remove and shred them (having taken cuttings for stock) and

One of the glories of Boveridge is the Long Walk with its herbaceous borders designed by Gertrude Jekyll. Some of the lovely plants that soar and jostle there today, such as *Achillea filipendulina,* were not on Miss Jekyll's original planting lists. Faithful, full-scale restoration, necessary to eradicate ground elder, will mean a return to her planting scheme of some eighty years ago.

start again once the ground has been cleared. The stone retaining wall behind the border is also harbouring the pest. On closer examination it could do with rebuilding.

One way or another, this is a project that must be done bit by bit, section by section. The plan is to clear the ground completely, replace the contaminated soil and replant. At a ballpark figure of something like £200 per foot (30cm) this will take quite some time and hundreds of thousands of pounds. But – encouraged by Chris Beardshaw's enthusiasm – Boveridge has decided to bite the bullet and seek grant funding and all that entails. Watch this space.

Plants and stonework combine happily in the gardens at Boveridge House. *Ricinus communis* 'Impala', however, was not in the original planting lists and will have to go in the cause of authenticity.

Sources and References

Norton Priory

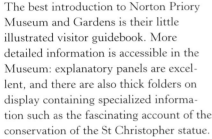

The best introduction to Norton Priory Museum and Gardens is their little illustrated visitor guidebook. More detailed information is accessible in the Museum: explanatory panels are excellent, and there are also thick folders on display containing specialized information such as the fascinating account of the conservation of the St Christopher statue.

I was treated to personal tours and pertinent answers to questions from the dedicated staff, including Steve Miller, Lynn Smith, John Budworth, Paul Quigley and Sarah Barwick.

It's always good to know the practicalities of the past. An invaluable reference book for what people ate when is C. Anne Wilson's *Food and Drink in Britain* (1973, paperback 1991). An oblique sidelight on thirteenth-century medicine from secular Wales is provided by *The Physicians of Myddfai* (facsimile reprint, 1993). To remind myself of aspects of the historical background to the herbs story I still turn to my well-worn and familiar Herb and Spice Book by Sarah Garland (1979) as well as to more recent books by herb guru Jekka McVicar.

The BBC team helped me especially with transcripts of Chris Beardshaw's interviews with Anthea Boylston and Alan Ogden of Bradford University, and shared the research supplied by Judith Palmer on medieval medicinal herbs.

Croome Park

Our bible here is *The Coventrys of Croome* by Catherine Gordon (2000). Apart from the biographical material, the author's principal focus is on Croome's rich architecture, but her chapter VII entitled 'The Grave Young Lord and his Grand Design' documents the garden and landscape during this key period. She, too, draws on William Dean's ghosted 1824 guidebook An historical and descriptive account of Croome d'Abitot. As head gardener he must have been responsible for the hands-on 'Hortus Croomensis' appendix, but some of us would like to know the identity of the eloquent FRIEND.

As an antidote to received opinion, Tom Williamson's *Polite Landscapes* (1998) is essential reading for anyone investigating this period. For the plantsmen and nurserymen of the eighteenth century, my sources include Berkeley & Berkeley *The Correspondence of John Bartram 1734–1777* (1992), and *Hortus Collinsonianus*: an account of the plants cultivated by the late Peter Collinson by Lewis Weston Dillwyn (1843).

Personal help came from from Jamie Whitehouse and Martin Barton at the National Trust office at Croome, and staff at the Croome Estate Archives, especially Pip Wilson and archivist Jill Tovey. The BBC team provided a transcript of Chris Beardshaw's meeting with Nick Haycock, and it was good to share John Trefor's interest in and investigations into eighteenth-century nurserymen.

Bridge End Garden

A key source was 'Bridge End Gardens: Historic Landscape Survey and Restoration Management Plan' prepared by Liz Lake Associates (1999), which gathers together much of the scattered documentation. I am grateful to Martyn Everett at Saffron Walden Library, where among other items I was able to peruse the booklet *Bridge End Gardens* by John Bosworth and Tony Collins (1983), and Christine A. Plumb's article on 'The Gibson Diaries' in *Saffron Walden History*, No 36, Autumn 1989.

John Bosworth, Restoration Project Manager, is indomitable in sending out progress reports to interested parties grateful to him for reading my text. Ben Smeeden gave me a welcome first introduction to the garden. Tony Fry has been helpful in personal communications and via the BBC's transcript of his interview.

On the Quakers as gardeners see Arthur Raistrick, *Quakers in Science and Industry* (1968 edition); R. Hingston Fox and *Dr John Fothergill and His Friends* (1919).

My first awareness of the neglected heritage of urban parks came via two entertaining lectures by Stewart Harding of the Urban Parks Forum to the Welsh Historic Gardens Trust. His ideas are summarized in *Urban Green Spaces Taskforce– Green Spaces, Better Places* (2002). Tom Williamson's *Polite Landscapes* (cited re Croome) provides interesting insights into the decline of the first wave of English topiary gardens in the eighteenth century. Among his sources is T. Hamilton *Forest Trees: Some Directions About Raising Forest Trees*, ed. M.L.Anderson (Edinb. 1953).

Château La Chaire

Greenway

Boveridge House

Again the primary document is the in-house 'Historic Landscape Survey and Restoration Plan' (May 2003) compiled by Nicholas Pearson Associates, which draws together a considerable amount of biographical material about Samuel Curtis and the fortunes of the La Chaire estate since his ownership.

Besides A.B. Burleigh, 'Samuel Curtis FLS 1779–1860' in Journal of the Royal Horticultural Society pp.324–8 (1933), the DNB is useful for cameos of Curtis and his contemporaries, including Clara Maria Pope and her husbands. She – and Curtis's Botanical Magazine – also appear in Wilfrid Blunt & William &. Stearn, *The Art of Botanical Illustration* (1994 edition). On the florists see Ruth Duthie, *Florists' Flowers and Societies* (1988).

The infectious enthusiasm of Angie Petkovic' and Tony Russell deserves to be rewarded, and I wish them the best of luck. Good neighbours at La Chaire include John Brewster (who kindly shared his 'millennium history' of the parish of St Martin, Jersey with us), and Lady Guthrie: their gardens give us some idea of what can be achieved in the Vallée de Rozel. Rachel Ransom generously sought out and shared some of her research on Curtis and his garden with us.

On the Channel Islands context staff at La Société Jersiaise and the Jersey Archive have been helpful. At the Royal Jersey Agricultural and Horticultural Society, Pam Laurens endured an interruption on a busy day, while Derrick Frigot and James Godfrey gave me such interesting insights that I came away with a copy of their *Jersey's Rural Heritage* (2001).

An excellent starting point is the National Trust's 'Greenway Garden Survey' by Katie Fretwell and Melissa Simpson (December 2002), with its comprehensive documentation of Greenway's past owners and their family connections. Dr Audrey Le Lievre's excellent article 'Greenway' in *Hortus*, no 25, spring (1993) merits publication in its own right.

I also received much help – and a most rewarding personal guided tour – from Gardener Nick Haworth.

Besides Thomas Mawson's own autobiography *The Life and Work of an English Landscape Architect* (c.1927), an excellent introductory article is 'Thomas H. Mawson' by David Mawson, his grandson, in the journal *Landscape Design for August 1979*.

Works on and by Gertrude Jekyll are legion. Richard Bisgrove and Penelope Hobhouse are recommended reading, as is Jane Brown's *Gardens of a Golden Afternoon* (1982). The chapter quotes excerpts from Gertrude Jekyll, *Colour Schemes for the Flower Garden* (1982 edition), and the Goldalming Museum kindly allowed us to examine her notebook for Boveridge.

At Boveridge Lesley Walter and Alison Smith shared their enthusiasm and their research.

Some General Reading

Ray Desmond, *Dictionary of British and Irish Botanists and Horticulturalists*, Taylor & Francis 1994
Maggie Campbell-Culver, *The Origin of Plants*, Headline 2001
Brent Elliott, *Victorian Gardens*, Batsford 1986
John Harvey, *Medieval Gardens*, Batsford 1990 edition
Penelope Hobhouse, *Plants in Garden History*, Pavilion 1992
David Jacques, *Georgian Gardens*, Batsford 1990 edition
Mark Laird, *The Flowering of the Landscape Garden* 1720–1800, University of Pennsylvania Press 1999

Index

Illustrations are indicated by *italic* type.

Picture Credits

Norton Priory: p.13 plan, Stefan Kawecki; p.18 family crest by kind permission of the Brooke family p.19, 22 by kind permission of Norton Priory Museum and Gardens; p.20 perspective plan c.1770, Yale Center for British Art, Paul Mellon Collection/Bridgeman Art Library.

Croome Park: p.39 based on first edition Ordnance Survey 1884, overlaid with planting details from Snape's survey of 1796 and Hopcraft's survey of 1810 supplied by P. M. Owen courtesy of the National Trust; p.40 John Snape survey of 1796 by kind permission of the Croome Estate Trust; p.42 portait of George William Coventry by Allan Ramsay courtesy of the Croome Estate Trust and the National Portrait Gallery, London; p.43 portrait of Lancelot 'Capability' Brown by Nathaniel Dance by kind permission of the National Portrait Gallery; p.44 landscape with Croome Court by Richard Wilson supplied by kind permission of the Croome Estate Trust; p.57 nursery bills and p.60 facsimile of letter by kind permission of the Croome Estate Trust.

Bridge End Garden: p.67 plan by kind permission of Elizabeth Banks Associates; p.69 garden regulations Saffron Walden Library; p.72 portrait of Francis Gibson courtesy of William Gibbs; p.73 book plate courtesy of Tony Fry; p.85 and p.88 the Dutch Garden in early 1900s, Country Life Photographic Library; p.87 Gertrude Jekyll drawing of Dutch Garden taken from *Gardens for Small Country Homes*, Gertrude Jekyll and Lawrence Weaver, 1912, republished as *The Arts and Crafts Garden* by the Antique Collectors Club in 1997.

Acknowledgements

The first thanks are due to the BBC Wales team whose researchers discover innumerable hidden gardens and find a selection of the most exciting case histories for Chris Beardshaw to probe. Their briefing of Chris and myself is always superlative. The subsequent dialogues, adventures and explorations we share are the best part of the job. Special thanks to John Trefor, Jacci Parry, Ros Hatcher and Jeanette Minns, and to the cameramen and soundmen who add to the fun.

Thanks to staff at Norton Priory Museum and Gardens; the National Trust at Croome Park and Greenway, and the Croome Estate Trustees; to everyone involved in restoring the Bridge End Garden at Saffron Walden; to the small dedicated team working to restore La Chaire, and to staff and pupils at the Philip Green Memorial School, Boveridge.

Photographer Rowan Isaac has worked his usual wonders with the sky and the light to reveal what is not quite hidden about the gardens in question, and been good company in the meantime. Thanks to the patient book team of Pippa Rubinstein and Judith Robertson – fun to work with – backed up by Robin and Lisa at Cassell Illustrated.

Many people have helped and advised, but the opinions expressed in the book are the responsibility of the author alone.

Chateau La Chaire: p.93 plan APT Marketing Solutions; p.95 portrait by courtesy of Hampshire County Council Museums Service; Chateau La Chaire 1877 courtesy of Hampshire County Council Museums Service; p.105 letter from Samuel Curtis, private collection; p.109 portrait of Crown Princess Victoria Ka'iulani of Hawaii by permission of Picture History.

Greenway: p.121 plan courtesy of the National Trust/Creative Media; p.127 Edward Carlyon plan, Devon Records Office 1891B/P1; p.128 pictorial cartouche of Greenway House, Devon Records Office; p.132 ferns from *The Fern Garden*, Shirley Hibberd, 1879; pp.140–41 camellia pictures, slides taken by Frank Lavin, Head Gardener at Greenway by kind permission of Mr and Mrs Hicks; p.143 portrait of Agatha Christie, Walter Bird/Getty Images.

Boveridge House: p.149 plan, Stefan Kawecki; p.152 portrait of Gertrude Jekyll by courtesy of the National Portrait Gallery; p.153 Thomas Mawson by permission of Cumbria Record Office, Kendal ref. no. WDB86; p.155 south façade courtesy of Thalia Gordon-Watson; p.162 Sundial Garden plan, the Gertrude Jekyll Collection (1955-1) Environmental Design Archives, University of California, Berkeley; p.164 notebook by permission of Godalming Museum.

While every effort has been made to trace present copyright holders, the publisher apologizes in advance for any unintentional error or omission, and will be pleased to insert the appropriate acknowledgement in any subsequent edition.

Norton Priory Museum & Gardens
Tudor Road, Manor Park, Runcorn
Cheshire WA7 1SX
Registered Charity: 504 870
Telephone 01928 569 895
E-mail info@nortonpriory.org
Website www.nortonpriory.org

Directions From M56, take junction 11 and follow brown signs. All other directions, cross Runcorn/ Widnes bridge and follow brown signs.

Admission £4.25 adult; £2.95 Child/Concession; £2.50 group (10 plus); £10.00 family. Award-winning Education Service – ring for details.

Open Daily from 12 noon, all year round. Ring for closing times.

NORTON PRIORY MUSEUM & GARDENS

GREENWAY GARDEN
(National Trust)
Churston Ferrers, Brixham
Devon TQ5 0ES
Telephone 01803 842882
Bookings and Info Line
E-mail
greenway@nationaltrust.org.uk
Website www.nationaltrust.org.uk/
devoncornwall/greenway

Directions All visitors must pre-book their parking space. Greenway is entered through the village of Galmpton. Take the A3022 towards Brixham and turn in to the village. Follow signs for Greenway passenger ferry and quay. The property is 1½ miles down from the village off Greenway Road. Visitors are encouraged to visit by Green Transport, information from riverlink 01803 834488

Admission Visitors arriving by car £3.90; Child £1.95. Green visitors (foot, ferry, hopper bus) £3.25, Child £1.65.

Open 3 Mar–9 Oct Wed–Sat, 10.30–5.00pm

GREENWAY GARDEN
(NATIONAL TRUST)

CROOME LANDSCAPE PARK
(National Trust)
Builders Yard,
High Green Severn Stoke,
Worcester WR8 9AR
Telephone 01905 371006
Fax 01905 371090
Email
croomepark@nationaltrust.org.uk
Website www.nationaltrust.org.uk

Directions 10 miles south of Worcester. Signposted from A38 and B4084, between Upton on Severn and Pershore.

Admission £3.50 Adult; £1.70 Child; £8.50 family; National Trust members free.

Open 5 Mar–31 Oct, Wed–Sun & Bank holiday Mondays: 10am–5.30pm. 1 Nov–19 Dec: Wed–Sun: 10am–4pm.

■ Worcester

CROOME LANDSCAPE PARK
(NATIONAL TRUST)

Cardiff

■ Oxford

■ Bristol

Harlow ■

London ■

BRIDGEND GARDEN
Uttlesford District Council,
London Road,
Saffron Walden,
Essex CB11 4ER

Contact Tourist Information Saffron Walden, 1 Market Place, Saffron Walden, Essex CB10 1HR
Telephone 01799 510444
Fax 01799 510 445

Directions Direct access can be gained from the Castle St. or Bridge St. entrances. Car parking is available nearby at Swan Meadow car park or at Caton's Lane car park.

Admission Free. Open during daylight hours – please phone for further information.

BRIDGEND GARDEN

leave the village. After 1.5 miles, the entrance to the school is on the left. Follow the drive around to the left, this will bring you into the turning circle in front of the main entrance.

Open Gardens are officially those of Boveridge House and open only on Garden Open Days. 2004: 3–4 Apr; 3–4 Jul; 7–8 Aug.

BOVERIDGE HOUSE
Cranborne, Wimborne,
Dorset BH21 5RU
Telephone 01725 517218

Directions The Philip Green Memorial School.
In Cranborne drive through the village, follow signs for Damerham not Boveridge. You pass Cranborne Middle School on your left as you

BOVERIDGE HOUSE

LA CHAIRE
Sub-tropical Garden,
The Old Shop, Rozel Bay,
St Martins, Jersey JE3 6AJ
Telephone 01534 861231
E-mail info@lachaire.com
Website www.lachaire.com

Open La Chaire will be open from Spring 2004 for guided tours, booked in advance for 12 or more people. Bookings can be made exclusively through Compass Holidays on 01242 250642. There is no public parking adjacent to the garden. Alternative arrangements are in operation – please ask when booking.

not to scale